THE MIRROR THEORY

BETSY OTTER THOMPSON

THE MIRROR THEORY

The Way to Inner Peace, Resolution, and Transformation

HAMPTON ROADS
PUBLISHING COMPANY, INC.

Cover design by Marjoram Productions
Cover digital imagery © 2004 PictureQuest. All rights reserved.

Excerpt from *Bloodline of the Holy Grail* by Laurence Gardner © 2001 is reprinted with permission of Fair Winds Press, 33 Commercial Street, Gloucester, MA 01930.

Excerpt from "James's Relationship to Jesus" chart from p. 25, and text excerpts from pp. 168–9, 207–8 from *The Brother of Jesus: The Dramatic Story & Meaning of the First Archaeological Link to Jesus* by Hershel Shanks and Ben Witherington III, copyright © 2003 by Biblical Archaeology Society. Reprinted by permission of HarperCollins Publishers Inc.

Excerpt from "Family Tree" chart from *Jesus and His World* by John J. Rousseau and Rami Arav, copyright © 1995 Augsburg Fortress. Used by permission.

Approximately 100 words (pp. 58, 81) from *The History of the Church from Christ to Constantine* by Eusebius, translated by G. A. Williamson, revised and edited with a new introduction by Andrew Louth (Penguin Books, 1995). Copyright © G. A. Williamson, 1965. Revisions and new editorial matter copyright © Andrew Louth, 1989. Reproduced by permission of Penguin Books Ltd.

Excerpts from *James, the Brother of Jesus* by Robert Eisenman, copyright © 1997 by Robert Eisenman. Used by permission of Viking Penguin, a division of Penguin Group (USA) Inc.

Hampton Roads Publishing Company, Inc.
1125 Stoney Ridge Road
Charlottesville, VA 22902

434-296-2772
fax: 434-296-5096
e-mail: hrpc@hrpub.com
www.hrpub.com

If you are unable to order this book from your local bookseller, you may order directly from the publisher. Call 1-800-766-8009, toll-free.

Library of Congress Cataloging-in-Publication Data

Thompson, Betsy Otter, 1936-
  The mirror theory : the way to inner peace, resolution, and transformation
/ Betsy Otter Thompson.
     p. cm.
  Summary: "A guide to improving your life based on the premise we are drawn or repelled by people who reflect both our negative and positive values. Each chapter includes questions and exercises featuring a different member of Jesus' family and illustrates central themes including blame, envy, and humility, helping you to improve personal relationships and advance spiritual growth by accepting responsibility and seeing your emotional self in those around you"--Provided by publisher.
  Includes bibliographical references.
  ISBN 1-57174-438-X (alk. paper)
  1. Interpersonal relations--Religious aspects--Christianity. 2. Jesus Christ--Family--Miscellanea. I. Title.
  BV4597.52.T46 2005
  158.2--dc22

                                        2004024274

10 9 8 7 6 5 4 3 2 1
Printed on acid-free, recycled paper in Canada

A considerate son
A loyal friend
A brave and courageous soul
Thanks, Bill
For being
Who you are
As you are
Where you are

Contents

Acknowledgments

Many thanks to
Lauri Vierra, Richard Krevolin,
and Mary Embree for their editing along the way.
Thanks to Shianna Kuhn for her ever-present support;
to Lisette Larkins, the angel who found me;
to Richard Leviton and Robert Friedman for their editing skills;
and to Charlie for his continuing wisdom and encouragement.

Family Tree

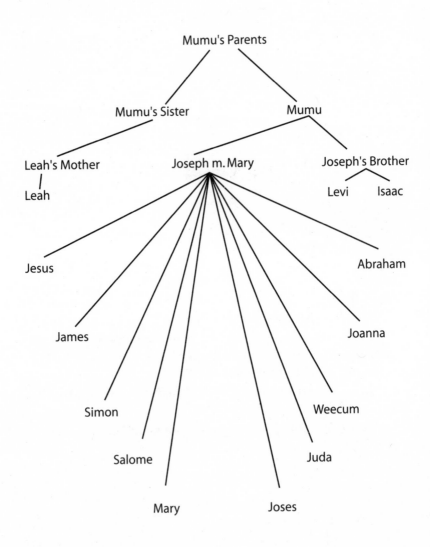

Preface

How many times have you met someone who changed your life completely? This is what happened to me seventeen years ago. My life was a mess. Not only had my second marriage failed but I had no money, no steady job, and no reassurance that things would improve. My family and friends were still back East and I had moved to California on the urging of some mysterious inner voice for which I had no reasonable explanation. I was alone, confused, and unhappy. For the umpteenth time, I was asking myself—what is my life all about?

Financially, I was surviving as a temp. Emotionally, I was surviving in the mode of blame, i.e., if only my mother hadn't screwed me up so badly, I'd be happy, successful, and well adjusted. I felt like a failure compared to my sisters and friends. Here they were living the lifestyles all of us had been brought up to expect— marriage, family, and fulfillment—and doing it successfully as far as I could see. I had tried and done miserably. Two marriages and four children later, I still had no peace of mind. Something was missing, something I couldn't name that felt vitally important to my survival.

What do I need? I thought. What do I want? What keeps me so defeated while others leap ahead? I tried everything I could think of: moving away from the problem, moving toward inspiration, reading books, getting therapy, trying EST; I conformed, I rebelled; nothing worked. I was tired of crying, tired of blaming, and tired of trying.

Poverty was eating away at my soul and desperation was taking over. On an afternoon in June of 1987, I was looking out the window, thinking that life couldn't get any worse when a knock on the door interrupted my thoughts.

There stood a man I'd never seen before—an older gentleman of average height and build, with gray hair, a rather engaging face, and eyes that kept me riveted. Dressed casually in slacks and shirt, he wore the oldest looking sandals I'd ever seen. I'm no fashion plate, but I knew retro when I saw it. He introduced himself as Charlie, an old friend of a friend. Before I could ask him what friend, he said to me:

I know of that inner voice urging you to move to California, and although you're struggling now, your life is about to transform because you were here to answer this knock on your door.

I stood there open-mouthed, aghast. How did he know? I hadn't told anyone. Who was he? What was he doing here?

Sensing my confusion, he said, *I know your life isn't working on many levels and I have a solution.*

I finally found my tongue. And convinced he was offering a pyramid scheme, I started to close the door and said, Sorry, I don't have any money to invest right now. . . .

I'm not referring to financial investments, he replied gently, *I'm referring to emotional investments. It's called the Mirror Theory and if you apply this theory to every part of your life—financially, emotionally, and physically—every part of your life will transform.*

I'd heard pitches before, but he was promising the moon. I

would have closed the door if my life hadn't been such a mess. But it was a mess, an awful mess, so I asked him where he'd gotten this theory.

It was given to me many years ago, he said, *by someone who came to me as I have come to you. It turned my life around as it can for you as well.*

I wanted a turnaround, that's for sure, but I'd tried everything and the only help I'd found was temporary. So I asked Charlie why his theory was any different from all the other self-help programs out there.

It's different because it's revealed through a story about Jesus and his brothers, sisters, cousins, parents, and grandmother.

Jesus didn't have siblings, I said. I went to Sunday school.

Indeed he did have siblings, Betsy, the old man responded. *But don't trust me, do some research.*

In the back of my mind I wondered how he knew my name. But distracted, I asked him why I should care about siblings, even if he had any?

Because they used the theory, too, and were deeply affected by their own transformations.

You must be talking about a very powerful theory, I said.

I am, but the power behind it comes from the powerful way these people used it.

What were their names? I asked.

When you're ready to know them, their names will be revealed.

Is the information different from what I already know about Jesus?

It's different in several ways, but it's a story that will thrill your heart and keep you asking for more.

I wanted Charlie's words to be true because I wanted my life to improve. He was offering hope and it made me realize how devastating my life had been without it. I asked Charlie how he'd relay this theory if I agreed.

I'll tell you the story as it was told to me. Then you can share it with others if it proves helpful.

Is it important that people believe these stories, Charlie?

No, it's only important that people love the stories they do believe in.

Love is the bottom line, Betsy, always—which is what the Mirror Theory helps you to realize.

What does the Mirror Theory refer to?

Emotional action/reaction. Everyone you encounter is an emotional mirror of the love or the lack of love you express. In fact, they reflect back to you a part of yourself. When you love what you feel from these mirrors, you think of life as grand. When you hate what you feel from these mirrors, you look for someone to blame. Dissatisfaction only comes from not working in a positive way with the part of yourself revealed. When you see everyone as a mirror and therefore a teacher, you free yourself from a victim mentality and gain a sense of gratitude for the answers right in front of you. Healing then becomes possible because the only thought that needs to be healed has been revealed.

Can you give me an example? I asked.

Sure. Let's suppose you are patronizing another. You may not be aware that you are; nevertheless, the emotional action is out there. If someone patronizes you and you feel offended, that's a sure sign that you have committed the same offense.

What happens if I haven't patronized another and I'm patronized?

You won't react to that behavior. In fact, you might not even notice it. And if you do notice it, you won't care.

Can you tell me more about the story? I asked.

It's a chronicle of Jesus' life and those who lived beside him, but it's also a program of spiritual self-help and guidance through which many people, regardless of their religious beliefs or lack thereof, can find inspiration and comfort.

Will Jesus be portrayed as more human than I'm used to seeing him?

Perhaps, Charlie said. *His family perceived him as just another sibling, who grew from a child, to a young man and adult. And in the eyes of God, all are equally loved, equally wise, and equally knowledgeable of the individual path that is needed.*

Will the theory be able to help me with my everyday problems?

It helped me with mine. Many issues will be discussed; the power of prayer, parent-child struggles, insecurity and self-esteem, the true nature of divinity, the concept of pain and suffering, the constructive use of money,

*and how to create more personal boundaries in a loving way. By the end
of the story, I wouldn't be surprised if you're asking yourself: Did Jesus live
a martyred path, make a conscious choice, stage a successful public rela-
tions event, or experience something else entirely? But regardless of your
conclusion, the goal is to make you aware of the love of God in you.*

Why have you come to me with this story? I asked.

*I knew you were looking for answers and since I had a few I thought
might help, I'm here.*

How did you know I was looking for answers?

I felt it, Charlie said.

Can I ask questions while you're telling the story?

Sure, Charlie said, *I welcome them.*

What if I ask stupid questions?

*There are no stupid questions. The purpose of our sharing is to find
the answers that work for you. Therefore, all of them are welcome.*

I may have feelings I want to express.

*I'm sure you will. Jot them down. Then if you share these stories with
others, they can commiserate with you.*

Are you sure it will be commiseration?

*That's how it worked for me. These people were human, too. While the
picture they lived may look different from the picture you are living, the
emotional struggles are universal.*

Were his family members different from each other?

*They all had reasons for being a part of that family, and they all had
different growth because of it. As the narrator, I'll convey their stories to you
to the best of my ability. You'll repeat the stories to the best of your ability and,
together, we'll develop a style of delivery that works for the common good.*

My meeting with Charlie was just as he predicted it would be:
a new beginning financially, emotionally, and physically. No words
can express my appreciation to him for his ever-present mentor-
ing, constant accessibility, and unending patience with me as well
as the project. I thank him over and over for inviting me to partic-
ipate and he thanks me over and over for joining his effort.
Perhaps you'll have a similar experience to the one I've had—one
that blesses your life, as every part of mine feels blessed.

The Research

In the following research, the sequence in which I found the information is not necessarily the sequence in this book. Nevertheless, the arrival of it was perfect for *The Mirror Theory*. What I discovered from delving into the past both surprised and delighted me. If your understanding of Jesus' story grows from what I learned, then I am doubly grateful. Keep in mind that every person who has researched this topic is trying to find answers. We all go about it differently and we all reach conclusions that bring us the clarity we seek.

First I looked in the Bible.[1] I found that siblings in general, as well as specifically, are mentioned.

> Is this not the carpenter's son? is not his Mother called Mary? and his brethren James, and Joses, and Simon and Judas? And his [Jesus] sisters, are they not with us? (Matthew 13:55–56)

Is not this the carpenter, the son of Mary, the brother of James, and Joses, of Juda and Simon? and are not his sisters here with us? And they were offended at him. (Mark 6:3)

In Matthew, the name Judas is used, while in Mark, the name Juda. In Matthew, the word "brethren" is used; in Mark the word brother—although both verses refer to the same event, almost word for word. The *American Heritage Dictionary* defines brethren as the plural archaic of brother. Some scholars have argued that Jesus used brethren to signify all people, not blood brothers. Perhaps that was true when Jesus was speaking. In these two instances, Jesus is not. If Matthew meant humankind for brethren in verse 13:55, why does he say brother in the same context in the following verse?

While he yet talked to the people, behold, his mother and his brothers stood without, desiring to speak with him. (Matthew 12:46)

Other Bible verses can be cited as well.

These all continued with one accord in prayer and supplication, with the women, and Mary the mother of Jesus, and with his brethren. (Acts 1:14)

But other of the apostles saw I none, save James the Lord's brother. (Galatians 1:19)

After this he [Jesus] when down to Capernaum, he, and his mother, and his brethren, and his disciples: and they continued there not many days. (John 2:12)

Galatians uses the word "brother" while the book of Acts and John use "brethren." If brethren designated all mankind, why is brethren and disciples identified separately in John 2:12? Perhaps brother and brethren were interchangeable, just as eternal and everlasting are for us. I believe the text is literal and the words mean exactly what they say. Quite a few other Bible verses speak of siblings,[2] which says to me that their presence was important.

Note in the Book of Matthew:

> And knew her not till she [Mary] had brought forth her firstborn son: and he [Joseph] called his name JESUS. (Matthew 1:25)
> And she [Mary] brought forth her firstborn son . . ." (Luke 2:7)

The Gospels were written after Jesus' life. Therefore, the word "firstborn" would seem to denote that Jesus was the first of other sons born of Mary. Otherwise, wouldn't it say, the son born of Mary?

Scholars have openly argued that Jesus had siblings, and many have openly argued for those Bible verses to be taken literally. Tertullian (c160–c225) in *Against Marcion* (verse 4.19) wanted a literal translation of Matthew (13:55–56) where the mother and brothers are waiting for Jesus.[3]

Hershel Shanks, in his book *Understanding the Dead Sea Scrolls,* mentions that James the Righteous is referred to in the New Testament as the brother of Jesus.[4] Millar Burrows in his book *Burrows on the Dead Sea Scrolls* speaks of how James is referred to as the Lord's brother in Galatians 1:19.[5] Flavius Josephus, the ancient historian says in his book *Antiquities of the Jews,*

> . . . so he assembled the sanhedrim of the judges, and brought before them the brother of Jesus, who was called Christ, whose name was James, and some others . . . (Chapter 20, verse 9.1)[6]

More recently, Laurence Gardner in his book, *Bloodline of the Holy Grail: The Hidden Lineage of Jesus Revealed* says,

> When Jesus became the David, his brother James became the Joseph.[7]

It's no secret that Mary had other offspring, as confirmed in each of the Gospels.[8]

In John Rousseau and Rami Arav's book, *Jesus and His World*, a
family tree is presented as the Line of David, and lists Jesus as having four brothers—James, Simon, Joses, Juda—and two unnamed
sisters.[9]

The Panarion and Ancoratus of Epiphanius lists three sisters for
Jesus: Mary, Salome, and Anna (Joanna).[10]

Hershel Shanks and Ben Witherington III wrote *The Brother of
Jesus: The Dramatic Story & Meaning of the First Archaeological Link to
Jesus & His Family*. The evidence for Jesus having a brother by the
name of James is partly based on an ossuary (a stone burial box for
the temporary storage of a loved one's bones) discovered in May of
2002 in Jerusalem with the inscription "James, son of Joseph,
brother of Jesus." Its authenticity is not one hundred percent
agreed upon within the archeology community but many noted
experts do accept it. Whether it proves to be genuine or not, the
possibility of siblings is firmly established in the minds of most who
studied this stone. Shanks, noted scholar and author, as well as edi-
tor of *Biblical Archaeology Review*, *Bible Review*, and *Archaeology
Odyssey*, along with Witherington, a prominent expert on the historical Jesus and a New Testament scholar, wrote this book about
James based on that validity. Andre Lemaire of the Sorbonne wrote
the foreword for Shanks' book. An article by Lemaire titled "Burial
Box of James the Brother of Jesus" was published in the
November/December 2002 issue of the *Biblical Archaeology Review*.[11]
When other archaeologists became interested in the ossuary, a
furor arose over its legitimacy. The article was then reprinted in the
November/December 2003 issue of the same publication.[12]

Shanks presents four explanations for the relationship
between James and Jesus through four different family trees. The
first has James, Simon, Joses, Jude, Salome, and Mary as blood
brothers and sisters. The others have various explanations
depending on which branch of Christianity supports that particular theory.[13]

Witherington also argues for the Gospels to be taken literally when referring to James as the brother of Jesus. He uses the writing of the ancient historian Flavius Josephus, mentioned previously, to further his point.

> The first thing to notice is that Josephus calls James "the brother of Jesus," just as in the New Testament and also on the ossuary. The term used here is *alelphos*, not the Greek word for cousin [some scholars have argued that James was a cousin], and this independent testimony to the relationship of James to Jesus is both early and important. Josephus called Jesus the so-called *(legoumenou)* Christ but does not call James the so-called brother of Jesus. Thus, it was not just early Christian writers who called James the brother of Jesus. This early Jewish historian did so as well.[14]

At the end of his argument for this literal translation, Witherington writes,

> As we have seen, the most natural explanation taking into consideration the Jewish context out of which the Gospel stories arise, and taking into consideration the narrative logic of each of the Gospel accounts, is that Jesus had several siblings, four brothers and two sisters, and probably the oldest of these was James. These were probably children of Mary and Joseph born after Jesus was born.[15]

Eusebius (c260–c349), an ancient historian, wrote *The History of the Church.* Much of his history was based on writings by Hegesippus (c110–c180), another ancient historian.

> . . . turned their attention to James the Lord's brother, who had been elected by the apostles to the episcopal throne at Jerusalem. (Book 2:23)[16]

Jude is also mentioned in Eusebius' book as a brother of Jesus.

> . . . a group of heretics accused the descendents of Jude—the brother, humanly speaking, of the Saviour—on the ground that they were of David's line and related to Christ himself. (Book 3:19)[17]

Robert Eisenman, professor of Middle East religions and archaeology, director of the Institute for the Study of Judeo-Christian Origins at California State University, Long Beach, and Visiting Senior Member of the Linacre College, Oxford University, wrote *James, The Brother of Jesus: The Key to Unlocking the Secrets of Early Christianity and the Dead Sea Scrolls*. His opening statement in his introduction states the tenor of his study:

> James the brother of Jesus, usually known as James the Just because of his surpassing Righteousness and Piety, is a character familiar to those with some knowledge of Christian origins.[18]

In many thought-provoking passages, Eisenman argues for the presence of brothers and sisters besides James, and also infers that James played a more prominent role in the furtherance of Christianity than previously believed. In the following two quotes, he reveals his position that many facts about Jesus' family were deleted from the Bible because of the goals of those who edited it.

> It should not be surprising that the existence of an actual brother of Jesus in the flesh was a problem for the theologian committed to an a priori doctrine of divine sonship or the supernatural birth of Jesus Christ.[19]

> This resulted in the downplaying of Jesus' brothers and close family members, including so-called "uncles" and "cousins," until they were finally all but eliminated from the tradition.[20]

In the first quote below, Eisenman refers to verses in Matthew and Mark, and comments. In the second quote, he reiterates his position.

> In the Gospels—primarily the Synoptics—we have the testimony to and the enumeration of the brothers of Jesus, however downplayed these may be. (Matt. 13:55; Mark 6:3) No embarrassment is evinced about the fact of these brothers. Nor is there any indication that they may be half-brothers, brothers by a different mother, or any other such designation aimed at reducing their importance and minimizing their relationship to Jesus.
>
> In these reports Jesus' mother and brothers come to him to talk to or question him. They are four in number, James, Simon, Jude, and Joses. One or more sisters are also mentioned—one specifically named Salome. (Mark 15:40)[21]
>
> For a start, let us reiterate that the initial stories about the brothers of Jesus in the Gospels—what Paul calls "the brothers of the Lord"—show no embarrassment whatsoever about the reality of the "brother" relationship, that is, whatever and whoever Jesus was *he had brothers.* That he also had a mother should be self-evident. He also seems to have had a "sister" or "sisters."[22]

Eisenman mentions the presence of Joanna and Salome in various scriptures as they bear witness "to the empty tomb and bearers of the rumour of his resurrection."[23] The sisters' relationship to Jesus is tied in with Mary, as she is identified as the mother of James in other verses, James is identified as the brother of Jesus, and the sisters are mentioned with James.

> There were also women looking on afar off: among whom was Mary Magdalene, and Mary the mother of James the less and of Joses, and Salome; (Mark 15:40)
>
> And when the sabbath was past, Mary Magdalene, and

Mary *the mother* of James, and Salome, had brought sweet spices, that they might come and anoint him. (Mark 16:1)

Luke adds Joanna as being present.

It was Mary Magdalene, and Joanna, and Mary *the mother* of James, and other *women that were* with them, which told these things unto the apostles. (Luke 24:10)

In this verse, Joanna is married to Herod's steward, which fits in logically with her role in *The Mirror Theory*.

And certain women, which had been healed of evil spirits and infirmities, Mary called Magdalene, out of whom went seven devils. (Luke 8:2) And Joanna the wife of Chuza Herod's steward, and Susanna, and many others, which ministered unto him of their substance. (Luke 8:3)

Evidently, a man of position in Biblical times could have several names. Laurence Gardner in his book, *Bloodline of the Holy Grail: The Hidden Lineage of Jesus Revealed*, writes:

Within the Judaean kingly, priestly, angelic and patriarchal successions, there were numerous dynastic and hereditary titles, along with various distinctions of office and appointment. Thus it was possible for any senior individual to be known by a series of different names according to the context of the moment. As we have seen, Matthew [in the Bible] was also Levi in his official capacity. Zacharias was the Zadok and was, therefore, angelically Michael. Jonathan Annas (sometimes called Nathanael) was also James of Alphaeus (the Jacob of the Succession), but additionally he was the Elias.[24]

Because one person could have several names and different people could have the same names, and because of the frequent repetition of names out of popularity and family connections, it's difficult even for biblical historians to agree upon which person is being identified. Eisenman says,

> There is a collateral aspect to this welter of like-named characters in the New Testament—even going so far as to include "Mary the sister of" her own sister Mary (John 19:25). These instances are all connected with downplaying the family of Jesus and writing it out of Scripture. This was necessary because of the developing doctrine of the supernatural Christ and the stories about his miraculous birth.[25]

The biblical number of siblings is close to the number in *The Mirror Theory*. Abraham and Weecum, two additional brothers in this book, lived through circumstances setting them apart, which could explain their absence from other versions. Although Shanks lists two sisters because he knew that at least two existed from the Bible, *The Panarion and Ancoratus of Epiphanius* lists three: Mary, Salome, and Anna (Joanna), which corresponds with *The Mirror Theory*.

Introduction

I know you must be asking yourself, why haven't we heard about relatives before? I don't know why, but if enough people ask a question, an answer comes. Haven't you ever wondered about Jesus' family? And haven't you known others who have, too? Isn't it possible that lots of people in the last two thousand years have wondered as well? Maybe some of them felt an answer but lived in a time that wasn't conducive to hearing it. Would this information have been tolerated a century ago? Perhaps this story is manifesting now because the hearts on Earth are open to receiving it. And perhaps it doesn't matter if you believe this story is real or not. Perhaps it only matters that you feel what is real in your story.

The only thing I know with absolute certainty is that using the Mirror Theory has changed my life, demonstrating that feelings aren't done to me inadvertently, but as a reflection of all that I have given. I'm not saying I always love those mirrors, but at least I have an explanation for why they are with me.

From this awareness, I've been able to see my mistakes as hard-earned growth and my shortcomings as eventual blessings. The message has given me a clearer vision of who I am, why I'm here, and how to accomplish my goals. It has helped me to enjoy more tolerance for human frailties, respect for inner strengths, and compassion for all that I've tried in the name of love. The feedback it offers has put me in a position of power to re-create.

The truth of action/reaction has motivated me to let go of blame for I've seen how it all comes back to me in others. It has helped me to find answers for why I get sick and advice on how to heal. It has helped me to accept that *timing*, or the moment something happens in life, is a specialty of the soul. It has helped me to understand that my happiness depends on how I view life, and it has given me proof that I am not a victim of other people's behavior. It brought me the realization that my biggest challenges have been my greatest gifts. More importantly, the message has taught me to appreciate the criticizers, for they have forced me to look deeper into myself for the truths I came here to live.

Understanding the Mirror Theory and how it works has been a gradual process. First I had to admit that life was not the *happy ever after* I anticipated. Then I needed the willingness to work hard for improvement. From this one act of faith, the universe rushed in with my mirrors to help me do it. Not that I always recognize that help when it arrives. Plenty of times I don't. But if I take responsibility for my emotions, that leap of faith is possible.

I know now that mirrors don't stop appearing simply because I refuse to deal with them. My soul is too invested in my choices to abandon me under pressure, and your soul is equally invested. But each of us moves inward at our own comfortable pace. For that reason, the meaning of this book is personal. The stories can be taken literally, symbolically, or both. Life is subjective; perception individual. My guess is that your assessment today will depend on what is happening in your life now, and your assessment in the future will depend on what is happening to you then. In the years

I've been writing this book, lots of ideas have been clarified, but new ideas are always presenting themselves with the need to be clarified.

Noticing mirrors resembles the art of pole vaulting. The low bars are easy to negotiate; the higher ones more challenging. Happily the higher ones come when the easier ones have been mastered. Usually, as I've gotten better at mastering the easier ones, the harder ones have begun to look easy.

Don't be surprised if your soul has more faith in your abilities than you do. This essence believes in the rightness of every leap. Have patience, trust yourself, and appreciate the heights to which you have already stretched your unlimited imagination. Be thankful that you have come to this Earth at a time when so many loving messages are being heard from so many different souls through so many open vehicles.

Don't be concerned if it seems that all those around you are living their mirrors and you aren't. That's the first sign that a giant leap of faith is happening; you are seeing the Mirror Theory at work. This is your soul's way of reassuring you that, yes, mirrors are alive and well and waiting for you to embrace them. You'll see them as soon as you remember that you don't come here to be perfect; you come here to remember that you are perfectly fine the way you are.

May you live wisely, in a loving heart full of grace.

Using This Book

There are several ways to approach *The Mirror Theory*. My recommendation is to read it cover to cover, doing the worksheets at the end of each story.

The chapters all have specific themes. For example, in chapter 9, Mumu, Jesus' grandmother, talks about her need to control others to such an extent that she alienated the very people she loved. In chapter 13, Abraham, Jesus' brother, talks about his embarrassment regarding Jesus, not because Jesus wanted to cause friction, but because of different needs. In this respect, you can choose the chapter that's relevant to your life in the moment. If you're feeling like a control freak, or someone you know is acting like one, go to Mumu's chapter to find a healing. If someone in your family is making embarrassing choices, go to Abraham's chapter for consolation. Because of the individual themes in each chapter, *The Mirror Theory* also works as a reference book. One day,

Mumu will have the help you need, another day Abraham, and likewise for all the chapters.

Regardless of how the book is used, you'll find what you need. In fact, you could open it randomly, and still find the exact page, with the exact message, that suits your needs in the moment.

When you come to the worksheet section, take your time. Whether you need an hour or a week to find your answers, do what is comfortable. Be whimsical. Keep your sense of humor. The point of each worksheet is to bring the ideas from the book into your everyday life in a meaningful way. These exercises can inspire more truth in you, help you to trust your path, and awaken your appreciation for all that you've lived so far.

Glossary of Terms

God: All that exists—sometimes singular, sometimes collective, always living in oneness

Reality: All that you feel

Illusion: Anything not felt

Love: Everything you are

Pictures: The game of matter

Ego: Anything blocking the flow of love

When the word *who* takes precedence over the word *that*, it is intentional. It is done to help you realize how personal life is.

Focus is the creator,
Determination the follow-through,
Completion the reward.

1

Mary: The Headstrong Mother

Heaven has no timid souls.
Heaven is
A belief that
Boldness is you.

Are you saying, Charlie, that boldness describes the personality of Mary?
I am. She made bold choices at a very young age—even when they created circumstances she had to live with for the rest of her life. In fact, her willfulness had a great deal to do with her growth in general.

Is boldness a good quality?

That depends on whether you notice the good it wrought. Happily, Mary eventually saw the advantages of her choices. Quite a few of them brought her heavenly feelings.

Perhaps Mary had a better chance of feeling them with a son like Jesus.

Perhaps she had the same chance you have since heaven is found through release.

Release to what?

What do you want to be released to, Betsy?

Living life as I see fit.

Give this release to others and it's yours.

Did Mary have trouble releasing Jesus?

She certainly did, mostly because Jesus talked half the day away about God, the universe, and eternity. Mary wondered how he'd ever handle his Earthly needs—that is, unless he joined a religious order. When he shied away from the only direction that held any interest—the temple teachings—she pushed him to do what she had done in hopes that he'd find the same contentment she had.

What about his carpentry skills?

Jesus never took them seriously. He preferred to think of himself as an orator. Mary didn't see how he could become one in the world in which he functioned. He had no political ambitions and that's where she saw speakers making their mark. Instead of settling down and making what she thought were sensible choices—like getting married, having children, and planning a career—he was off getting involved with the many heretical nomads roaming the land and preaching revolution. Mary was beside herself. She referred to these people rather condescendingly as *haggais*, a name that was given to self-proclaimed prophets and which, like your word mentor, had gained generic meaning through over use.

To her they weren't respectable. She had higher ambitions, wanting Jesus to succeed more conventionally, and she wasn't the least bit shy about telling him so. He was well aware that he had some decisions to make. He just wanted to make them comfortably and not under a lot of pressure. Although he fell back on his carpentry when he realized that he'd have to support his Earthly needs like the rest of humanity, he didn't start out with woodworking as his lifelong ambition. He was convinced he was destined for holier pursuits.

Wasn't he?
Only after he realized the holiness of carpentry.

Did Mary hope he would get married?
She did. She was a strong-willed woman who thought she knew what was best for her children and who, for years, did her utmost to make her influence felt. In her opinion, a good wife would drill some sense into him—her sense, that is—but Jesus would have none of it. He dragged his feet with one excuse after another as to why it wasn't right for him. Had Mary listened to him more carefully, she would have realized that Jesus wasn't ready for a step like this. He was restless, and had a short attention span about anything that didn't interest him. When something did, his pursuit of it was unstoppable. The women Mary knew wanted a devoted family man who would support and nourish that unit.

Not that she knew what Jesus needed, she didn't, but she wanted to. So she pushed him to do what had satisfied her, in hopes that he'd find the same satisfaction. Mary's dream of happiness was to have a big wonderful brood to love and to cherish. Jesus didn't want a family, at least not in the conventional sense. He had a broader vision of kin. Mary's struggle came from refusing to accept his point of view as valid. But she didn't want it to be valid since she'd invested much of her life in a different one. When Jesus fought her on this issue, she became even more determined to prove her reasoning right.

Life hadn't been easy for Mary. In fact, the beginning of her marriage had been fraught with drama, almost more than she could bear. She certainly didn't want her children living the same discomfort she'd experienced from stepping beyond society's dictates. Even though she eventually found contentment, her pain was well remembered. God forbid that her children suffer likewise. Therefore, in what she considered everyone's best interests, she presented a conservative approach to life and did her best to push her children to live it. When it looked like Jesus had other ideas, she was distraught. How was he going to find "the good life" if he didn't seek one? How was he going to avoid the pitfalls of snap decisions if he didn't live discreetly? How was he going to survive without the normal precautions everyone knew were wise?

Mary cared so deeply because of her own missteps, becoming pregnant without the benefit of marriage and having to cope with the consequences. Her mind had little to do with what happened, however. She got swept up in emotion, the exact situation she didn't want for her children. She loved Efie, the man who had sired her child, and she thought he loved her. When faced with the news of her pregnancy, he decided differently and disappeared. Unwed mothers were not treated kindly in her community. In fact, they were often lucky to survive. One of Mary's relatives by marriage had not. The best that a woman could hope for was to suffer the shame she brought upon her family. Mary knew she'd have to find a man who was willing to marry her and find him fast.

Joseph lived nearby and had always been attentive. Although she hadn't thought of him as a possible mate before she knew he'd thought of her that way. Since it looked like it was going to be Joseph or no one, she told him her whole sad story. He said he would marry her but it wasn't an easy decision. Joseph had loved her from afar, always knowing that Mary wasn't interested. When all of a sudden she acted like he was the answer to her worst nightmare, his pride was injured. Nevertheless, his respect for self and love for her were potent enough to overrule any nagging doubts, and they wed.

Did an angel come to Mary on a roof and tell her she'd bear the Son of God?

Mary found an angel but not on any roof. She went to her in a fit of panic when she thought she was pregnant. This woman told her to find a husband immediately if she didn't want to suffer the pain and humiliation that a righteous, God-fearing community would rain down upon an unmarried pregnant woman.

The Bible says that Jesus was the Son of God, not man.

Everyone is the Son of God since everyone is spirit in reality and human in illusion. It's just that people began to think of Jesus as special at the end of his life because he understood the nature of spirit so well. But he was conceived the same way you were.

Did Joseph's family support his marriage?

He didn't discuss it with them before the fact. After the fact, they had plenty to say. As far as they were concerned, Joseph had made a fool of himself. And Mary had made her own social blunder by accepting his offer. But Mary had a dilemma. How could she explain that she'd married a man below her station simply because she'd been foolish enough to chase a man above her station? She was headstrong but she wasn't stupid. She couldn't think of any good reason to be honest since nothing would change if she were. But Joseph was willing to trust her integrity regardless of the trouble she'd gotten herself into. He was also willing to believe that his need to be happy was more important than his need to please his elders.

Although Mary had known Joseph on a casual basis for years and always respected him, love was longer in coming. First, she had to stop fretting over what she'd lost and appreciate what she had. Efie had awakened the passionate side of her nature and for that reason alone was hard to forget. Joseph turned out to be a kind and thoughtful husband, a devoted father, and a true and caring friend. Mary quickly learned a broader meaning for the word love.

Efie eventually returned only to learn that Joseph and Mary had

5

married and left town. Mary didn't see him again for years. They reconnected after Jesus returned from solitude when Efie heard a rumor that a man called Jesus was performing miracles and healing the sick. Upon learning that Jesus was the firstborn child of that union, he was sure he was the father. Then he began to think that perhaps he'd made a mistake by disappearing before. Here was this son of his making quite a name for himself as a healer. He wanted to share in all that glory.

When he found Mary, he apologized for losing his courage all those years before. There was nothing to forgive as far as she was concerned. Mary had long since made peace with his decision. In terms of her pregnancy, she knew that both of them were responsible. More than any aggression on his part, her willfulness had brought it about. She was determined even in those days. But she did have worries: *What am I going to say to Jesus? How will Joseph handle this development? Will my children think less of me? Will Efie talk to others? Will he be believed?*

Mary had every fear that a woman in this situation could possibly have but the terror only came from her own lack of faith. As soon as she realized why fear was stalking her, she talked to Jesus. He heard her out, took her in his arms, and said how glad he was that she had found the courage to tell the truth. Jesus assured her that from that moment forth the burden would end and the truth would be a blessing.

Surprisingly, Jesus accepted this revelation easily. With a keen sense of self and a keen sense of all that pertained to his life, he suspected something like this already. But he did the same thing with this information he'd been doing all along—nothing. Together, Joseph and Mary told the rest of the family. Each child handled it differently, but all were supportive and sure that the strength of their union would see them through any threatening crises. None developed because as soon as Mary brought the facts out into the open, there was nothing more to fear. Efie did what he'd come to do: get to know his son. Jesus welcomed him with the same friendliness he gave to everyone because by then, Jesus saw everyone as family. Mary was delighted, too, because a potentially bad situation had turned into a miracle.

The presence of another man besides Joseph is not the story most people know, Charlie.

What makes sense to you? If Joseph were the man who had fathered Mary's child and everyone accepted that, would she have left the nourishment of family and friends and gone off to heaven knows where in the middle of her pregnancy with nothing to show but the clothes on her back? She needed a strong motivation to push her out of the nest I assure you. She was young, and while she was smart enough to know how to help herself, she wasn't any seasoned warrior.

Did Mary and Joseph leave their home because of feeling threatened?

No, they left because her family ignored their marriage and his family bombarded them with criticism. They decided that a new start would benefit their union.

Hadn't there been prophecies that a king would be born to threaten the present reign?

Prophecies of a king being born had little relevance to Mary and Joseph. The mentality in those days ruled out any possibility of a king rising from the likes of them. And kings weren't thought of in any other reference.

Did Mary's family believe that Joseph was the father of her baby?

She wanted them to. But before they eloped, no one even knew she was friendly with Joseph. Efie, however, had been around all the time. Her parents were greatly pleased by his presence for they favored such a union. What do you suppose they asked themselves at this point? *Where is Efie?* of course. No one knew. Rather than quarrel and debate the issue, Mary said she loved Joseph. The alternative was to admit to having married a relative stranger in order to save face. She wasn't secure enough to reveal any such thing.

The idea of Jesus' conception as earthly is also different from other stories.

Do you believe that Jesus was earthly?

I believe he lived a life here on Earth.

Perhaps that's the only proof you need that he was the same as everyone else.

The Church teaches that Jesus was special because he was the son of God.

Then that makes everyone special in the same way.

But he did things that others can't do.

All have the same potential.

Could Mary do what he did and bring people back from the dead?

Jesus only brought himself back from this illusion.

He healed many, didn't he?

He showed people how to heal themselves by letting them see inside his heart. When they looked, they saw their own health and wholeness. Eventually, Mary loved herself enough to consider that she was the same beautiful energy in a different disguise. Then she did some healing, too, later in life.

When Jesus was a child, Mary had many different feelings about him, and while she always loved him dearly, there were times when she thought she'd go crazy if she had to listen to him talk for another second. He needed a constant audience for his ideas. And if he couldn't find one at home, he'd go where he could find one.

Mary wasn't the only one he irritated. Most of his relatives lost their patience at one time or another. The little ones didn't mind so much. They loved being greeted with such enthusiasm by their older brother. But regardless of who was bothered by whom, Jesus brought a talkative nature because the presence of it was an important part of his path. As with many gifts, the early stages of development were quite trying on others.

Jesus knew of Mary's annoyance. She was always vocal about it. Sometimes he reacted to her admonishment; sometimes he acted as if she hadn't even spoken. His reaction depended on his behavior, too. If he'd been patient with others, he wasn't annoyed by her impatience. If he'd been short with others, he felt her shortness acutely.

What do you call this phenomenon—of emotional action causing emotional reaction?

I call it physics in a general sense, or, what goes around comes around. Later in life, Jesus called it doing unto others as you'd have them do unto you. In this particular venue, I'm calling it the Mirror Theory.

Did Jesus ever talk to Mary about this theory?

Upon his return from solitude, he did. Before that, he talked about anything he thought important. In fact, Jesus never let up with the questions. He exhausted both Joseph and Mary. When they were queried out, he approached other family members, even his younger brothers and sisters, hoping they'd say something useful. When their enthusiasm paled, he challenged his friends. When their answers didn't satisfy him, he turned to the safest rabbi.

The safest rabbi—what does that mean?

It means that some of the rabbis were unapproachable and wouldn't dream of taking time out of their day to answer a child's questions. Jesus chose carefully in this respect and, happily, that connection kept him busy for years. This rabbi was thrilled with Jesus' curiosity and loved it when the younger generation showed an interest in temple traditions, but even he grew tired of Jesus' constant confrontations. The rabbi, much to his relief, had another source to fall back on—the enormous library the temple offered to those who wanted to study the past. This particular focus monopolized his youth, and eventually Jesus left home because even the temple with its volumes of information had run out of satisfying answers.

When he told Mary he was leaving, she had mixed emotions. On the one hand, she didn't want him to go because he was a treasured member of the family; he was also a business associate of Joseph's. On the other hand, she understood his temperament well. She knew that if he didn't pursue his goals, life with him would be miserable anyway. Therefore, with a reluctant but trusting heart, she wished him well on his journey.

He wrote frequently, and although the mail system was hit or miss in those days depending on the traveling patterns of those who were carrying it, a lot of his letters got through. He wrote of his many adventures and Mary didn't think he was finding anything new that he hadn't found at home. By then, however, she knew that Jesus had his own path to follow whether she thought it wise or not. She finally accepted that when it came to career, mating, and social position, areas of interest that captivated his brothers and sisters, Jesus was unconcerned and unmotivated.

Jesus never rebelled for the sake of rebellion, though. His needs were well thought out. If you wanted to argue with him over what he considered important, it was wise to know your subject beforehand. He kept himself well informed about anything relevant to his path. If it wasn't relevant, he abstained from the conversation, sometimes to the point of rudeness, but rude or polite, he had his reflection to remind him of his behavior.

Are you talking about an active reflection or a metaphysical reflection?
I'm talking about an emotional reflection—one that is felt, not one that is necessarily seen.

Did Jesus use the concept of the mirror in his teachings?
He used the concept of emotional actions reflecting back to the giver.

How did Mary see Jesus as he was growing up?
As a person striving to be a peacemaker. When tempers rose over this or that, he only wanted the feuding parties to feel comfortable again. Since his motivation was altruistic, his help was usually appreciated. Not that his peace-making efforts didn't irritate others on occasion, especially when he thought that resolution could only come from discovering who was right and who was wrong. After he realized that right and wrong were arbitrary judgments, he asked the feuding participants to sit on the other side of the argument and be the other person—that is, if they wanted a

solution that worked for both of them. But Jesus acted like an agent go-between from the moment he was old enough to talk—a highly desirable trait in his particular path.

Did Jesus seem happy when he returned from traveling?

He seemed settled, if not completely content. It was more like he had a sense of what he wanted and knew what he was going to do about it.

Could Mary feel his intentions?

Yes, she could feel his aura the same way you feel the auras of others, especially those you know very well.

Did Mary think his previous travels had been wise?

She thought he'd found great wisdom from going, so, yes, she thought they were. But he was restless again very soon, and Mary wondered what that meant in terms of the future. Her answer came in the form of a prayer one night at the dinner table when he asked for patience in accepting the needs of others, prudence in accepting the will of others, and generosity in accepting the paths of others. Mary knew he was asking for the rest of the family to give him the same.

Teary-eyed, she asked what he had in mind for himself next. He said he was leaving again; this time, only as far as the hills. He needed solitude for the next journey was within. She understood how much he wanted guidance from God, but she still believed he could find it another way—hopefully in a way she supported. Mary repeated her old arguments, and while Jesus understood her feelings, he had his own to consider. After minor protestations from her and patient explanations from him, she realized he had something important to settle within and would have to do it his way. Therefore, she blessed his progress in hopes that her prayers would bring him home sooner. They didn't, but they made her feel better.

Why didn't they bring him home sooner? Aren't prayers powerful?

That depends on what you're praying for. Why would her prayer for Jesus to come back soon, override his prayer to stay as long as he needed? He had his own schedule and no prayer of hers had the power to counteract it.

At this point, their relationship had more to do with feelings than with time. As Jesus found renewed love for himself through introspection, Mary felt his renewed love for her. As those feelings grew, she stopped counting days, months, and years, and started counting blessed emotions instead.

How could Mary's emotions grow from what Jesus was doing?

Haven't you found growth from the doing of others?

Yes, but he wasn't sharing his journey with her then.

Oh, but he was—in the only way that mattered—through his belief in oneness and his love for her.

Could Mary feel him speaking to her?

There were times when she thought so, but whether she heard his voice or not, she could feel his heart expanding, and that was very inspiring.

How long does it take to reach this kind of knowledge?

Time is a tricky subject when it comes to enlightenment. Light is an ever-expanding thought. Therefore, embracing it isn't a matter of days, months, or years, but of how deeply the heart feels as they pass.

But I want to know how long it took so I can gauge for myself.

Each soul has its own schedule when it comes to enlightenment. Energy is imaginative in terms of growth. You have your way of expanding. Mary had hers, Jesus had his, and likewise for every soul who has ever graced this Earth with its presence.

Then how can I know the time it will take?

If every moment is appreciated in your quest to gain more knowledge, why does it matter?

When Jesus returned from solitude, did he move in with his family again?

Briefly, then he found a place where he could minister to others without inconveniencing the rest of the family. At this stage of his life he was content as well as settled. The changes were more about focus. Before, he'd been looking for ways to satisfy self. Now, he was looking for ways to share his satisfaction.

Who are you today compared to who you were twenty years ago, ten years ago, or even one year ago? You know yourself better, don't you? This was the change that Mary noticed in Jesus. But, at this point, he focused so intently on this one area of attainment that the process accelerated quickly. Fortitude can be applied to any number of goals; the reward being the mastering of those you choose. Mastering is mastering, regardless where it's directed—music, gardening, or within. Jesus' reward from knowing himself was to be in touch with his inner beauty and therefore in touch with the whole heart of God. When the whole is understood and embraced, you know everything the whole knows, then everything the whole knows is yours to enjoy.

Maybe he couldn't try for anything else because he didn't have any other talents.

Maybe so, and isn't that wonderful? He pursued what he did well instead of stewing over what he didn't. Therefore, what he did well grew. This Jesus was the same Jesus Mary had always known but, as he felt closer to himself, that closeness was contagious and couldn't help but rub off on others.

Did he seem faultless and without human failings?

He seemed full of love. He told Mary many times that human failings were only a few opinions we have about ourselves. We could choose to call them human strengths instead. More importantly, how do you define a human failing, Betsy?

As my inability to always love others.

Jesus said you didn't need to; you only needed to love yourself. And if you respected the many ways there were to love, self-love regenerated.

I make mistakes, Charlie.

Jesus said that mistakes are nonexistent since you make choices for the enlightenment of your soul. Therefore, whatever is chosen is meaningful toward that end.

Are you referring to a Higher Self?

The Higher Self is the you who always loves, and since this higher self never forgets its identity, you and your higher self are one when sharing that emotion.

I can't always remember this core in me.

A loss of memory doesn't weaken your position; it inspires new efforts. Be glad for the beauty you do remember and have compassion for the heart who is stretching so broadly. You are the beautiful love of God, acknowledged or not, so you might as well enjoy it.

Aren't you encouraging pretense?

Pretense is about acting as if you aren't the divine love of God, not acting as if you are.

Did Jesus tell Mary that he and she were one?

He told everyone this.

Did they believe him?

Do you believe me in the same context?

I want to think we are but I know I harbor doubts.

Jesus heard the same response. *I want to believe, but . . .* So he told people to doubt all they wanted to. In the long run, it wouldn't matter as long as they gave as they wanted to receive.

Sometimes I doubt if I'll ever see this world as a loving heaven.

Forget about the rest of the world and find this heaven in you.

I try to.

Do you succeed?

Sometimes.

Focus on your sometime successes instead of your intermittent failures; this is how successes grow.

Did Mary's life change after Jesus returned from solitude?

It was much the same in terms of the people she knew and the places she went. The biggest change was emotional. She saw what focus and commitment had done for Jesus and began to see what focus was all about. He had his goals. She had hers. Joseph had his. And all were equally important to the people living them.

Gradually, Mary stopped judging goals and respected the many different ones people had. As a result, she witnessed a great demonstration of the ripple effect. As Jesus honored himself, he helped her to honor herself. Her changed attitude encouraged her children to change theirs. On and on it went into ever widening circles of love. However, Mary had less faith in the outcome than Jesus did. She thought his decisions would be the death of him. He thought his decisions would be the eternal life of her.

Did he ever take Mary into his confidence more than he did other people?

As his mother, he brought his heart to her quite often, but Jesus was an open book to everyone. Eventually Mary learned to be open, too, by watching what happened to him from his openness. He showed her the difference between living to please others and living to please self.

You mean Mary watched how he pleased everyone else and then knew how to do it?

No, she watched as he tenderly cared for his needs and then knew how to care for hers.

Don't I get more holy by putting the needs of others first?

Since you can't get any holier than you are, the only game is to recognize holiness. This is what Jesus taught Mary to do: honor her divinity, thereby inspiring others to honor theirs.

What do you mean, we can't get any holier? Surely, some people have more goodness in them than others.

Some are more in touch with their goodness, but everyone has an equal chance to enjoy it. For Jesus to accomplish his ambitions and connect to the source of goodness in him, he had to learn to please himself. Denial couldn't get him any closer to universal power. The nature of wholeness is to be full, not deprived.

Did Mary panic when the negative threats came to Jesus at the end of his life?

She panicked when he ignored these threats. Against the advice of family and friends, Jesus continued to preach. Mary knew it was just a matter of time until the government took action. Hoping to delay the inevitable, she discredited his enemies. Therefore, she lived compatibly with other condemning hearts. Together they experienced what happens to the soul in mistrust.

It was hard for Mary to believe that even suffering was individually interpreted, but it turned out that what she feared, Jesus did not. He told her several times that just as mothering was her forte and something she understood well, his path was well understood by him. Just because she imagined it all as terrible didn't make it so. Some of his friends had more faith in his path than Mary could muster. She hadn't fully acknowledged her wisdom yet, so she couldn't fully acknowledge his. Nevertheless, Jesus felt her pain and realized how helpless she felt to control it, so he asked her to take a walk with him to further discuss her worries.

What did he say?

Let me answer your question with one of my own. What if you had plans for a wonderful trip and someone you loved didn't want you to go? What would you say to comfort him?

That my trip was important to me, that I had some dreams to fulfill, and that I would share those experiences upon my return.

This is essentially what Jesus told her.

Did Mary wonder how he could think this way in terms of a crucifixion?

Yes, and he said that he had often wondered how Mary could enjoy the presence of so many children. But his doubt hadn't hindered her pleasure in the slightest. When she asked him how he could compare the size of a family to pain and humiliation, he said that pain and humiliation were what he would have experienced had he tried to live her preferences. But since he had found the courage to pursue his own, he now wanted to share what happens when personal dreams are honored. When Mary asked him what would be revealed, he said it would be the power of love.

What about his love for Mary? He was making her suffer.

If you told your friend how wonderfully excited you were to be making a trip but he remained unhappy, would you be responsible for his misery?

No, he'd be responsible for his own feelings.

Mary wanted to trust that Jesus knew what he was doing. Granted, this was a big challenge. She told him how worried she was for his safety, and he said that he knew what awaited him and there was no safer place to be. When Mary mentioned the suffering he might find along the way, he said he was already there, and since the body understood what the mind had found, the body felt safe, too.

Are you saying that Jesus knew that he wouldn't suffer on the cross?

I'm saying that Jesus thought of pain and death as two separate beliefs and he didn't embrace either. He had reached his conclusions the same way Mary had reached hers and you have reached yours. For instance, how do you know that one day follows another?

I have lived that sequence.

Well, Jesus had lived what others thought was death and hadn't died. He had lived what others thought was pain and hadn't suffered. Therefore, he kept his own counsel regarding these truths. He discovered the properties of self while in seclusion. Therefore, whenever he wanted to return to those properties, he only had to remember the beauty of being in them.

All of life is energy. Energy is light, and light is love. I can't give you an earthly explanation for that which is emotional, but I can tell you that it isn't difficult to grasp. It can be difficult to live when you get distracted by what looks important to the eyes instead of what feels important to the heart.

What about Jesus living through pain and not feeling it?

Why does one athlete find health and prosperity as he pushes his body to the limit, while another finds pain and injury?

Training.

What is training?

Teaching the body to perform a certain task with nourishment and exercise to back it up.

Which is exactly what Jesus did. He took his body to where the mind already was through exercise and discipline.

What if I train my body hard but still get hurt and still feel pain?

Then you have misunderstood the nature of training. You are here to find the love in your path. If the body is well toned and ready to perform, but the mind isn't ready to love through it, the body won't hold up. The body is here to serve the God within. Therefore, when an athlete forgets the goal behind a trained body, the body forgets what it's been trained to do. Jesus stopped feeling pain when all he ever brought to his body was the love of God.

He felt no pain on the cross?

Can you imagine someone letting himself be crucified if he thought he would?

No one thinking clearly.

I couldn't agree more.

But I thought he suffered so that others wouldn't have to.

Do you learn to suffer from those who are suffering or from those who aren't?

What do you mean?

How do you learn to play tennis?

From someone who knows how to.

That's what I mean. How could Jesus teach the end of suffering if he hadn't ended his own? He didn't suffer on the cross. He showed us what happens when the soul merges with the conscious mind to know itself as the love of God in matter.

Didn't others hear him cry out for God to help him?

Mary was there and she only heard him speak of love and forgiveness.

Didn't he ask God to forgive those who had crucified him?

He allowed himself to be crucified so why would he blame anyone else? He could have stopped preaching, left town, and escaped the whole business. He was the one who considered crucifixion timely. Why would he ask God to forgive those who played along with his plan? He wanted the people to forgive themselves. Mary heard him say *love can never die and I will see you shortly to prove it.* He returned three days later to fulfill his promise. *I am here to show you what faith in yourself is all about* he said. *God is within. When you honor this essence, nothing can touch you, hurt you, or alter you. Mine this love and all that you are will join the everything there is.*

Did Mary believe he had magical powers?

How could she? She had raised this man from infancy and seen him through his struggles, lessons, and triumphs. He was the same in every way as all her other children except that he had a different goal. What he did seemed miraculous, but he assured them that whatever he could do, anyone could do. So naturally, people began to question the nature of miracles. Were miracles the natural way to exist and living without them unnatural?

People don't die and come back, Charlie.

Perhaps they do but it just isn't recognized as such. Mary had seen others do it in her lifetime and heard them speak of how wonderful it felt. It can happen to anyone if the oneness of light transforms the moment. ·

What does that mean?

What does it mean when a lamp is turned on in a dark room?

It means that the room becomes illuminated.

That's what it means. The light is turned on within and illumination is.

How can I live that way?

By loving your life. How you express your divinity is up to you. Holiness isn't something you have to find. You are this energy now. To know it is to honor the beauty within. We all have the same opportunity since we all come here with emotion and we all have the freedom to use it. God doesn't give a heart to one and ignore another. Love what Jesus lived if it makes you happy. But remember, he found his heaven on Earth because he honored what was right for him. To find your heaven, you must do the same.

Jesus got himself into the human game just as you have done. What he did after that is exactly what you're doing—living life as fully as possible. Yes, he lived a resurrection, but you live one, too, every time you choose to love. Just because your resurrection doesn't have the same look his had doesn't mean it's any less powerful. Both speak to the rebirth of love. Rebirth can happen any number of ways from the first breath you take on this planet to a resurrection such as Jesus'.

He lived in miracles.

Not always. He learned to because he refused to believe that anyone had more of a chance to live them than he did. A shift in thought is needed, a shift to the powerful autonomous energy within. Don't worry if you understand the nature of God. Think of God as love and live what it means to you. Then you'll find everything Jesus found.

Would you call Mary a supportive parent to Jesus?

She tried to be, but the path he chose often tested her patience. From the moment he was old enough to talk he was challenging authority—often hers. He didn't balk from any lack of respect, only from an insatiable curiosity about the world around him and a fierce determination to think for himself. As he grew older, it was only natural that the rabbis and politicians would see him as rebellious. They didn't want their ethics or policies threatened. True to form, Jesus stood fast rather than compromise his beliefs.

Joseph and Mary worked long and hard to establish themselves in the community and feared what his defiance would mean to the rest of the family. Not until Jesus returned from traveling was he able to relax and enjoy the many other ambitions that serve the soul on its journey here on Earth. By then, however, he understood where to go to satisfy his ambitions.

> There is no greater or lesser
> In the mind that embraces all.
> There is only wholeness
> Living to beautify self.

Worksheet for Chapter 1: Mary

Write down all the ways in which you are bold.

How has this boldness revealed more of your personality and the core that lives within?

Would your life have gone differently had you not engaged in boldness?

How can this boldness be used in the future to further reveal your strengths?

What boldness do you hope to continue to manifest? Feel all the ways you might encourage this beauty.

Questions to Ponder

• Am I responsible for how others behave or am I only responsible for how I react to that behavior?

• Do I welcome new connections or do I welcome new ways of keeping them at bay?

• Is my behavior leading me to, or away from, the unions I want to encourage?

> God is, God gives, God questions, God lives.
> Your origin, your now, your future, your forever.

Personal Insights

After hearing Mary's story and the choices she made, I thought about the choices I had made as a mother. And, of course, I was influenced by the mother I had. She made decisions, just as Mary made hers, from a conviction that she knew what her children needed. She wasn't always right just as Mary wasn't, but she wanted her children to be happy in the same way she had been. I rebelled against her pushing, and when I was a mother, I did the opposite. I may have gone overboard in the other direction, but my motives were the same as hers—for my children to have what they needed for living a happy life. These days, I don't ask myself if I was right or wrong; I believe that my children came here to experience the mother I was, just as I came here to experience the mother I had. And happily, I've had a better look into the heart of my mother from hearing how Mary struggled with hers.

2

Joseph: The Purposeful Father

Just because something is easy
Doesn't mean it is filled with joy.
Just because something is difficult
Doesn't mean it is joyless.

Is a purposeful attitude always desirable, Charlie?

That depends on how it's focused. Purpose can be used in the art of living skillfully or in the art of living painfully. Joseph's challenge was to use his nature productively and to trust the path he was on. He had some mighty good reasons for doing so. The main one being his need to accept, with grace, that he was Mary's second choice. Chosen under duress made the challenge even greater. Other struggles came and went but none as big as this one. It didn't get any easier from wishing things were different. It got easier from highlighting all the good reasons he'd married Mary in the first place and remembering all the love he'd found from doing so.

Mary tried to reassure him, but he could sense her heart and it almost broke his when he did. Surprisingly, her fondness for another was not the problem. She loved a lot of people and hoped to expand that circle. Joseph knew that she cared for him and he knew that she wanted the union to work. Still, he imagined comparisons.

For years he feared that she judged him according to what her eyes could see instead of what her heart could feel. The other man was handsome and Joseph was average. The other man was closer to Mary's age and Joseph felt ancient. The other man had money as well as social standing. Joseph had neither. He suffered greatly while struggling to overcome his dreadful fear that Mary was sorry for having to settle for him. Happily, she saw past the superficial and welcomed his love. But even after she relaxed and found contentment, he harbored fears.

Why?

Why do you, even when there is no reason to?

I hear a nagging voice that won't let me rest in peace.

Well you aren't alone in this predicament. Joseph heard it, too. Mary wanted him to feel secure in their relationship, but she couldn't force him to. She could only feel secure, hoping he'd sense her sureness and realize more of his own. Both of them had to focus on the positive aspects of their union, not on the might-have-beens. As contentment grew, you'd think that ego would have left him alone, but no, it was still there trying to be heard and still trying to get his attention. He finally stopped listening.

It's hard to stop listening. That voice speaks.

Maybe so, but during your lifetime many voices speak. You

25

don't have to listen to the ones you don't enjoy. The same is true for the ones within. Joseph thwarted that negative energy by thinking of all the good reasons he and Mary were together and remembering all the ways their union was blessed.

During that struggle, they had to contend with the fact that Mary's family thought she had married beneath her. And when they discovered she was issuing, they were scandalized. Deportment rules were rigidly defined in their community. Feeling that judgment deeply, Mary and Joseph decided to move away. I'm not saying they were run out of town in the literal sense. No one threw rocks at them or burned their home. But when you've been treated badly enough, long enough, you feel like it's happening.

They didn't handle that meddling well; partly because they tired of hearing how foolishly they had behaved. Mary didn't want to endure even greater shame by admitting to the truth. However, not admitting the truth invited Mary's relatives to treat Joseph like the cad they thought him to be, and Joseph's family joined in. Had they at least been honest, the families would have seen Joseph as a man who loved Mary deeply. In this respect alone their alliance would have improved.

He couldn't help Mary find peace while creating disharmony for himself. Eventually, he came to understand why they felt so bitter. It wasn't because he had so little to offer in the picture of abundance; it was because he had so little to offer in the honesty of his heart.

If it sounds like Mary wrapped Joseph around her little finger, it's true. He was willing to marry her even though she was pregnant by another, and whether she loved him or not. He was besotted. To him, marrying Mary was miraculous under any circumstances.

After they moved away and had more children, peace was declared and relatives came to visit. Each time they did, the warmth they encountered encouraged longer stays. Eventually, a brother, mother, and several cousins of Joseph's settled nearby. A softening of hearts occurred throughout the years and a mutual respect developed and grew.

It's strange to think of Jesus as having grandparents. Rarely has his humanity, in this respect, been focused on.

Then perhaps it's time that it is.

Did Jesus irritate Joseph the way he sometimes irritated Mary?

All children irritate their parents once in a while. This family's experience was no different from yours or anyone else's. They had all the normal struggles around discipline and learning.

Didn't Jesus have a special holiness that made Joseph want to leave him alone?

Joseph felt that all his children were holy. Jesus had his own unique personality but so did all the others. Before Jesus was born, Joseph wondered how he would deal with this aspect of parentage. After Jesus arrived, Joseph was besotted with him as well.

Why did they move so close to Mary's due date?

They didn't. They left with plenty of time to arrive at their destination. Joseph was concerned, though. His family had no money to spare, Mary's had disowned her, and he was poor. They could have gone to the synagogue for assistance but felt too proud to beg. Eventually they settled in a cave where Mary gave birth. She wasn't too happy about being there but everything turned out fine and Jesus was born. The friends they made were enormously helpful and proved to be a sturdy and loyal group of people, welcoming them with compassionate love and understanding. It turned out that as soon as they made some wise decisions for themselves, they found the same wisdom in others.

The Bible speaks of three wise kings bearing precious gifts.

There were several families with loving gifts to offer and Mary and Joseph thought they were very wise and kind, but they were simple folk, struggling to survive the same as they were.

Where did this other story come from?

Perhaps from someone's interpretation of what three wise men would look like and what three loving gifts would be.

Are you saying that the biblical story is symbolic?

Not exactly, I'm saying that love is interpreted individually. To Joseph, those with precious gifts were those with something Mary and he could use. But many people have heard this story, and many interpretations exist because of that.

What about following the star to find them?

Their friends didn't need any star to guide them. They knew where Mary and Joseph were. These newlyweds weren't alone in their poverty. They lived among those known as the hill people, and circumstances motivated them to look after each other the best they could. Perhaps it's a matter of asking what makes sense to you. Why would three rich strangers come to honor the birth of a baby in a cave to relatively obscure parents who were poor and new to the community?

Because they received news that something unusual was happening.

Why would the birth of a baby up in the hills be unusual?

Because God told them what was happening.

Even if that were so, all they would have heard was that another god had birthed into humanness. Why would they have bothered with theirs?

Because Jesus was special.

To Mary and Joseph he was, but Jesus' birth was no more or less important than yours or mine. Each new beginning is equally beautiful to the oneness from which we all source.

Did Joseph think God was guiding him?

When things ran smoothly, he did. When they didn't, he tended to think otherwise.

Did Joseph believe that God was running Jesus' life?

No more than he thought that God was running his. But God doesn't show favoritism. Each person is valued with equal enthusiasm.

Jesus came here as the person he needed to be for the journey he wanted to live, and you have done the same.

You mean God blessed him with what he thought a special soul deserves?

Jesus blessed himself with whatever he thought would reveal his own true nature, but God is the love in every dream. Whatever brings more meaning to each and every journey is the special gift embraced.

Yes, a Supreme Being led his way, but it's the same Being who leads your way. And because this supremacy knows itself as the everything in every moment, you only need to feel it in your dream and you are one. Just because you forget to love doesn't mean it isn't present. It's here because you are, but to be is one thing, to enjoy being is quite another.

It's hard to imagine this force within. I attribute such grandeur and power to it. How can I equate myself with divinity?

If God is the everything that exists, how could God be something you aren't?

I see the logic in it. I just can't see infinity in myself.

Can you feel it?

I can relate to the fact that thought has no boundaries.

Then surely it could have thought you up. It's only hard to imagine God when you think of it as something outside yourself, pulling the strings of your life. If you see yourself as an equal part of the whole to which all belong it's easy. Then it becomes a matter of understanding self, not some unfathomable concept.

Doesn't the ultimate God, who knows everything, see what I need and give it to me?

You mean this beautiful force in you?

I mean the one big God, Charlie. The one who IS all, knows all, and sees all. The one we pray to for help. Doesn't this God hear my prayers and answer them?

The one big God *is* simply the force within. Yes, this energy hears your prayers and answers them. It's just that consciously, you don't always acknowledge those answers when they arrive.

Why?

Because answers usually involve more love and forgiveness on your part.

Does this energy always have perfect eyesight?

Would a God who IS all have imperfect eyesight? And if this God always sees things clearly, wouldn't you have the same eyesight if you always saw things clearly, too?

I suppose so but who has that ability?

That depends on how you define "seeing things clearly." It means to see everyone as an equal part of the whole.

I do my best to be a good person but I'm not fool enough to think I'm God.

Maybe so, but God isn't fool enough to think that something exists besides energy. The extent to which you feel that beauty depends on the depth of your love. Even if you don't feel it every single second, so what? Is the ocean less of an ocean simply because it loses its ability to stay free of impurities now and then? And if not, why would God be less in other situations? Yes, I'm comparing humans to the ocean, but both are godly expressions so the same logic applies.

If everyone is the same clear-thinking God that Jesus was, why did he live in miracles and I don't?

Joseph asked that question, too. It turned out that he just wasn't open to what it meant to be thinking clearly. As soon as he was, miracles began. Clear thinking comes to the person who takes responsibility for who he is and what he has created, leaving blame behind—exactly what Jesus did. As Joseph watched

Jesus become accountable, he learned from example to do the same.

In Joseph's situation, taking responsibility was pivotal. It shifted his focus from that of a victim who was helpless to live anything other than that which had been meted out to him, to a person who could experience whatever he gave. As soon as he used this power to get what he wanted, what he wanted was more of this power.

If it's such a great idea, why isn't everyone living it?

Everyone is. Not everyone is aware that they are. In your own life, why do you blame instead of take responsibility?

It's easier to think of my problems as somebody else's fault.

That's why he blamed, too, but it was only easier the first few minutes. After that, he had the blaming of others to contend with. Then instead of living in clarity once, he lived in blame again and again.

He was full of bitterness. If Mary's family had only been more compassionate, if his had only been more trusting—if only this, if only that. I'm not saying that life had ever been perfect for Joseph, but never had so many woes arrived at once. Nevertheless, there he was, without any home, without any income, and with a wife about to have a baby. It was enough to discourage the bravest of souls.

Blame was so debilitating because it convinced Joseph that something was wrong. The feeling that something was wrong fed off itself and caused more negativity. When he stopped condemning the choices of family members and started finding pleasure in his own, joy had a chance to feed off itself instead. Mary and Joseph helped each other with as much bolstering as they could, and the more support they gave to each other, the more they attracted as a family.

As life improved, the need to expand in other ways took focus. One of them was to look for suitable lodgings. Then the challenge became to find the same contentment in his new abode that he'd found in the cave. To do so, he had to focus on the present instead of the past. The idea of finding a home was very appealing; the idea of leaving his friends was not. Happily, they stayed in touch with quite a few and continued to enjoy those friendships.

Did any of these people follow Jesus' career?

Absolutely. Several were still around when it blossomed.

How did Jesus get over the use of blame?

The way most people do—by learning what it created. He and Joseph had one of these lessons together. Jesus loved coming into his father's shop in the afternoons to discuss carpentry projects. Often Jesus was helpful if his skills were up to the task. His interest in woodworking created a bond with Joseph, who forever bragged about Jesus' creativity. The business bustled with activity and many were forced to listen to him.

There was never a formal agreement that Jesus would join his father after school, but the routine had been in place for years and both expected it. Then, unbeknownst to Joseph, Jesus became infatuated with one of the girls in the neighborhood and thought that being with her had a lot more appeal than coming home to be with Joseph. Because Jesus suspected he'd be teased or embarrassed in some way, he didn't share his plans. When he didn't show up, Joseph started to worry and set off to look for him right away.

His first stop was the park. When Joseph found him there, he was so irritated by what he perceived as Jesus' thoughtlessness, he had no consideration whatsoever. He marched right over to him in front of his peers, grabbed him by the arm, and insisted on knowing why he hadn't informed him of his plans. Instead of telling Joseph he was sorry, Jesus stalked off in a great huff.

Naturally, that made Joseph even angrier and he ordered Jesus home immediately. When they got there, Jesus was justifiably enraged and so was Joseph. No matter how long they argued, they couldn't resolve their conflict. Jesus hated his father's disrespect for his independence. Joseph hated his son's disrespect for his authority. As they argued, Joseph learned that independence to Jesus meant his right to make decisions regardless of his father's expectations. Jesus learned that authority to his father meant his respectful attention whether he wanted to give it or not. It took a lot of talking and a lot of listening before either one of them gained the needed perspective.

Joseph thought that Jesus should apologize for not telling him his plans; Jesus thought that Joseph should apologize for humiliating him. The conflict was about both but not in the way you might think. Jesus hadn't felt humiliated because of how Joseph had treated him. He felt humiliated because of how he'd humiliated his father. He knew how embarrassed Joseph would be in front of his customers when he didn't show up.

On the other hand, Joseph didn't lose authority because of how Jesus treated him. He lost it because of how he deprived Jesus of his. A youngster arriving at the age of puberty is entitled to make of a few of his own decisions. Joseph wasn't aware of how fast Jesus was growing and wanted to keep him the child he'd always known. Joseph hadn't been smart about his own adolescence and didn't think Jesus could be smart about his. The problem got resolved as soon as both of them acknowledged the discomfort the other must have felt.

Did they ever take their disputes to the rabbi?

They took disputes to the rabbi, but only when they couldn't resolve them otherwise.

Did Jesus want to be a rabbi?

He thought so once in a while, but as he grew older, he had few illusions about these men. He was more interested in learning about his predecessors. Jesus was often accused of being a cynic but he wasn't. He just blurted out his opinions when he had them. And his observations were closer to the truth than others wanted to acknowledge. With little patience for hypocrisy and a tendency to be open, he got himself into trouble, verbally disagreeing with those who considered themselves the ultimate authority—the rabbis and politicians.

Jesus was well aware of local politics from the time he was a child, as most of the children around him were. Their lives often depended on staying aware. He knew that any challenge in that direction would have to wait. The rabbis took the brunt of his rebellion. He got in trouble with the girls, too, by blurting out his feelings, whether the girls wanted to hear them or not. Then the girls retreated in embarrassment.

Jesus knew he wasn't handsome but he didn't think he was ugly. He just didn't understand why the right words for courting never came to him while the right words for everything else did. Eventually he saw how this inability to converse was a blessing. It gave him more time for his studies—and he was a very dedicated student. He even got to the point where he had a sense of humor about it. He once told Joseph that it was a good thing he wasn't irresistible to the girls or he'd never have time to challenge the rabbis so successfully.

His religious community didn't abide much controversy. As Jesus got older, his boldness made people uneasy. He was obsessed with finding answers and wasn't reluctant to confront those he thought were not taking him seriously. The elders, in their frustration, often expected Mary and Joseph to intervene.

Jesus was challenging honored beliefs and calling them wrong. Joseph thought he was stirring up a lot of trouble over nothing. He'd had similar doubts in his youth and so had many of his friends. Most of them had moved on and Joseph was sure that Jesus would, too. When he mentioned this possibility, Jesus said that he had many questions for which he had no answers, and he wouldn't stop his quest until he found them.

Unfortunately, when Jesus challenged the rabbis, people called him a heretic. That confused him. He wanted the truth. In his fervor to find it, he disdained the beliefs of others. Then others disdained his. Not until he returned from solitude did he have a comfortable rendering of truth: *each soul has a truth it needs.* Jesus was consistent in that he always preached what he believed in. But his truth evolved as he redefined himself.

After solitude, he was easier to be around. He'd stopped trying to convince others of anything. He was simply telling people to love whatever truth they had and watch it expand. He didn't see much of the rabbis then, but he didn't shun them either. He had faith that each soul knew where it needed to be and with whom it needed to converse.

How did Joseph feel about Jesus' preaching?

When Jesus came home from the hills, Joseph took more of an interest. Jesus had stopped talking about how wise he was and starting talking about how wise Joseph was. He found that refreshing. Also, he was in need of wisdom himself. Jesus' biological father had decided to acquaint himself with his son.

Was Joseph still insecure about Mary after all those years?

After all those years he had more reasons for wanting life to run smoothly. Earlier, Mary and he were the only ones who would suffer. Now he had a family to think about. In an effort to cope, he went to a meeting where Jesus was speaking. He heard him say, *fear is created by refusing to face the truth about our lives. But as soon as we do, fear disappears. It only lives in a soul that refuses to make a decision. To heal is to walk right into whatever we think is paralyzing us.*

Being a man of action Joseph took that advice and confronted the problem directly by asking Jesus' father why he was in town and what he intended to do. Instead of facing an enemy, he faced a person looking for resolution. Only his worry of what could happen kept him so off-balance. After he decided to deal with the situation regardless of the outcome, he found the comfort he longed for. When Joseph told Jesus he'd tried one of his ideas and found success, Jesus smiled and gave him a big hug.

Was Joseph worried in the final days of Jesus' life?

When the rumors of possible crucifixion started, he was. After talking to Jesus his worries abated. He knew that other people's anxieties often came unfounded. Granted, his own challenges were less conspicuous and certainly not life threatening, but many times he wondered how he'd ever survived the many dramas he had created. Nevertheless, he was happier and wiser for having lived them.

Why did Joseph trust Jesus' path while Mary did not?

Because, by then, Joseph trusted his own path. He also found it easier to be objective. Jesus was no fool, nor was he a martyr. He'd never given up a single thing that mattered to him. How could Joseph believe that Jesus had suddenly lost his senses? He had always made unusual choices; choices that no one else understood. Nevertheless, he was well adjusted, satisfied with life, and happy in his decisions.

Joseph found it impossible to think of him in any other reference. Jesus was more directed and focused than most of the people Joseph knew. He had complete faith in him, as several others did, too. Mary and Joseph both knew Jesus equally well, but faith doesn't come from knowing others well, it comes from knowing self well. Therefore Joseph had faith where she did not. Mary still doubted some of her choices. As she grew to value them, she found the same contentment Joseph had.

Did it take a long time for Joseph to feel secure in his relationship with her?
He began to feel secure as soon as he realized that he could either love their time together or he could fritter it away in fearful jealousy. Yes, his path was difficult. Not because of what happened to him, but because of how he handled it. As he doubted that true joy was possible, he expected pain. When it came, he took it as the natural way of things, expecting calamities where none existed— not a helpful tactic in terms of raising children. When dealing with Jesus, he had to accept that Jesus had candor to the point of curtness, honesty to the point of rudeness, and verbal skills to the point of annoyance. But as Joseph learned to respect Jesus' point of view, he relaxed more into his.

Joseph was driven by his ambitions. Jesus was driven by his. Both approached their challenges in ways that matched their growth. No one ever said that Jesus' position in life was great but he found greatness from appreciating where he found himself. Through his example, Joseph learned to love the choices he had made and to honor his life more wisely.

Power is never found from
Crediting others for what you have accomplished.
Power is found from
Believing in self.

Worksheet for Chapter 2: Joseph

How do you want your life to change?

What would improve if changes occurred?

How has your life improved because those changes didn't happen?

Who have you blamed for the circumstances you dislike?

How can you thank these people, instead, for the growth they forced you to live?

Questions to Ponder

• Who am I blaming for sadness that I should be thanking for growth?

• Am I resisting independence instead of embracing it?

• What do I know today that I wouldn't had life gone differently?

> If you want to see life as difficult
> You'll find plenty to support your theory.
> If you want to see life as easy
> You'll have to find some ease from living it.

Personal Insights

After hearing Joseph's story and the major challenge he faced: either to find the good reasons for marrying Mary or to wallow in self-pity, I took a deep breath. As much as I hate to admit it, self-pity took up a big chunk of my life—and I could have loved instead. I'm not proud of it. I could offer lots of excuses, but the fact is that I lived it with a vengeance. Why I kept that attitude for so long is beyond me. It never got me anything worth having. Maybe I thought when I died I'd be rewarded for suffering so much. I don't know. I only know that when I looked for the benefits and growth from what I had lived, my whole life turned around. I could probably say that I watched the Mirror Theory at work—meeting an optimistic attitude in others when I took one for myself—but I'd rather say it was simply a choice that put me in a better frame of mind and that was a miracle.

3

Levi: The Approval-Seeking Cousin

Nothing is more satisfying
Than standing up for self.
Energy in approval
Is energy in health.

How was Levi related to Jesus?

He was Joseph's nephew and cousin to Jesus. Before Joseph married, he spent a lot of time with Levi. He was fond of his brother's son, but as Jesus matured and battled with Levi over ethical issues, their relationship suffered. Not that he ever stopped admiring Levi's work ethic, he didn't. He admired it a great deal. What he did have trouble with was the grudge-holder in Levi. He was not a forgiving person when impinged upon inappropriately, and sometimes Jesus in his fervor for reform did exactly that.

Did Levi feel secure in his ambitions?

Most of the time he did, and when his faith faltered he looked for approval to get it back. Seeking approval didn't help much; it made him feel insecure.

What does security mean in the long run?

The same thing it means in the short run—emotional satisfaction.

Did Jesus interfere with Levi's sense of worth?

Levi thought so, but the feeling of worthiness comes from autonomous action to the betterment of self. This is something Jesus realized long before Levi did. And it certainly simplified matters because once he knew how life worked for him, he knew how it worked for everyone.

It's hard to have faith in oneself when going through difficult times.

True, but difficult times are the very incentive you need for gaining faith. Both Levi and Jesus struggled this way, Jesus more so in his youth, Levi later in life. Although they fought over many issues, they still saw one another at family gatherings and did their best to remain civil.

It wasn't until Jesus returned from solitude that Levi had any interest in Jesus at all. Before that, Levi saw Jesus as a self-appointed teacher; someone whose goal was to reform those in trade. With great defensive pride, Jesus would lecture Levi at every opportunity about how he was wasting his life. In those days Levi hoped that Jesus would grow out of this self-righteous stage and leave him alone.

Nevertheless, he had opinions about him at every stage of development. As a child, he saw Jesus as someone who was curious about his place in the world but unsure of his skills. As a young man, he saw Jesus as someone sure of his skills but not so sure about how to use them. As an adult, he saw Jesus as someone using his skills to help others find theirs.

Wasn't Levi curious about the miracles Jesus performed?

Yes, but Levi had his own miracles to consider.

How could Levi live in miracles if he wasn't living as Jesus did?

Miracles come in every size, shape, and symbol, and to anyone living happily. Why would Jesus be the only recipient of this form of insight?

Maybe we aren't defining miracles the same way.

Maybe we aren't. How do you define them?

As healings that transform one's life from disease and sickness to health and wholeness in the face of impossible odds.

If God is the epitome of health and wholeness, why wouldn't Levi's way of feeling healthy and whole be every bit as legitimate as Jesus' way? I'm not saying that Levi learned how to rise from the dead but he certainly learned how to rise from poverty and that was pretty miraculous to him.

You're teasing me, Charlie.

Only in that a broader sense of miracles will highlight those in your life.

Why would rising from poverty be a miracle? Lots of people do that.

The question to ask is why wouldn't that be a miracle if it seemed impossible? Isn't that how you defined a miracle? Miracles come to anyone breaking through illusionary barriers. The odds didn't look good for Levi in terms of obtaining wealth. But God doesn't deal in images; God deals in emotion. Therefore, as soon as Levi felt differently about himself, the picture reflected his growth.

What Levi thought he deserved wasn't necessarily what Jesus thought he deserved. Nevertheless, they each received what they made important. Going from poor to rich may not seem as enlightened to you as learning to rise from the dead, but God doesn't equate in terms of more or less important. God is every ideal and therefore considers all as equally valid. Wholeness doesn't rate any part of itself. Take your body, for instance. What would happen if you cut out one single part of it?

That depends. Some parts are more important—like the organs.
So you could function perfectly without the rest?

No, but surely I could do as well without a strand of hair here or a piece of skin there.
I'm sure you could temporarily but to think that you can get along without one little part here and one little part there encourages the message that you can get along without another little part here and another little part there. Soon, the whole is lacking a great deal of what it can be.

In principle, the *body of God* is no different from the *body of you*. Each part contributes to the whole. Favorites are unknown to an emotional force that only feels complete within itself. Jesus thought he'd feel better about his goals by making Levi feel insecure in his. But doubt is doubt regardless of where it's focused. The mind is a thought receptacle the same as a glass is a liquid receptacle. Whatever you pour into it affects everything else there. Jesus may have considered his goals worthier, and for him, that was true. But his goals wouldn't have brought much happiness to Levi.

Does that really matter?
Levi thought so. Aren't you entitled to live what you consider important? And if someone doesn't agree, does that mean you're wrong? Jesus may not have liked Levi's goals but he didn't know what Levi needed. And regardless of what Jesus thought, Levi had to find his own way back to love. He could only do that by approving of how he chose to live. Both of them were searching for love and both of them wanted meaningful lives. After Jesus released Levi to his ambitions, his own path opened up to the ones he favored. Fulfillment doesn't come from reaching your goals anyway. It comes from enjoying the process of reaching them.

If Levi focused on getting rich, how could he find the ultimate love that Jesus found?

He could because the ultimate love is appreciation of self. Look around you. God is living the ultimate wherever you see people loving their lives. Once you tap into that love, you want to expand it. No permanent state exists, however, where you wouldn't want to reach for more. God is a light that is forever growing in breadth and depth.

How can I reach perfection if it's always in a state of flux?

For that very reason. Perfection is simply the love you find in *the every moment* you exist. There is no other perfect to find. The ultimate for Jesus was the same as the ultimate for Levi, reflected by how much they appreciated themselves. For either of them to know this ultimate, they had to understand the game of life on Earth. That's what you're living, too—a game. Games have rules. They also have winners and losers, and techniques and strategies that either succeed or fail. Games offer satisfaction or frustration depending on whether you learn the rules and make them work for you. Once you understand how to play a game, that skill has then been mastered. The only difference between your skill in the human game and Jesus' skill is that he doesn't have to use the birth canal to play it anymore. You do. He remembers how it feels to be God in humanness.

As you remember that feeling, you won't need a birth canal anymore either. Jesus is not the only one who recalls this state. Many do, and every one of them is helping you to remember. But regardless of how well that feeling was known to Jesus while he was here on Earth, there are always more games in which to know it. Therefore, that's what he's doing: approving of self in other challenging endeavors.

He must wonder what's wrong with the rest of us that we can't get past this game.

Since you're in this one for the same reason he's playing his, I doubt it.

If he's playing another game, can he still respond to my prayers?

Yes, but the divine integrity that lives within all can do the same—regardless of where that soul exists—in-form or out-of-form. Even if this divinity is not acknowledged by you, the unconscious you is aware of it.

Are you saying that dialogues exist between those in-form and those out-of-form?

I'm saying that what you see with your eyes is illusion. The soul is real and eternal. Your soul has dialogues with other souls whether you're aware of it or not, whether you're in-form or out-of-form, and whether your body looks dead or alive.

When do these dialogues happen?

Constantly—asleep and awake. Sometimes you recognize them, sometimes you don't.

Did Levi learn about this ultimate, Charlie?

He learned that the ultimate could be felt in any thought one lived.

Would his life have been different had he known this truth much sooner?

No, the soul is always living to the depth of its imagination.

What was he hoping to grasp in his life as Levi?

The nature of wholeness.

The whole of himself, the whole of mankind, the whole of the universe? What whole?

Any and all. The same principle holds them all together: *Each part of the whole is an equal participant in terms of worthy emotion.* In other words, every part of the whole is equally holy, equally powerful, and equally capable of living a meaningful path.

What caused Levi's faith in himself to falter?

It happened because he believed that some people were more

important, more holy, more powerful, more autonomous, and more directed. That kept him thinking that he'd better join the more not to be caught with the less. But the constant pressure to have *more* kept him from being the most he could be for himself. You only have to remember that happiness doesn't come from knowing the ultimate details of another soul's life. It comes from knowing the ultimate in yours.

Then how can I know what to believe?

The same way everyone does. If a belief makes you happy, keep it. If it doesn't, release it.

Must a belief make me happy?

If there's a choice, why not? You're here to please yourself. Whatever you pour into the glass, you drink, like it or not, and anything tasting vile is hard to swallow.

When I leave this planet, what will I hope to remember?

Emotional satisfaction. You'll have no regrets about the actions of others, only what you forgot to do.

Do I live whatever I believe is so?

Yes, and those who believe as you do surround you like a shadow.

Are you using the word shadow the same as you use the word mirror?

Yes, in this discussion, they both represent an emotional reflection.

My shadow leaves when the sun goes down.

Your shadow never leaves you. You lose your ability to see it when you leave the warmth of the sun. Ignore that light and you lose your guide. This is what happened to Levi. He couldn't enjoy the love of the whole because he couldn't for the life of him honor those he thought less powerful, including Jesus. Not because he didn't like Jesus but because he didn't like what he represented—poverty, without the power to pull out of it. To him, Jesus epitomized lesser strength, and lesser strength threatened his sense of security. He heard a voice who said *he'll pull you down, he'll pull you down.* But Jesus was searching for power and approval, too. Each soul has its own way back to it, however, and Levi couldn't find his way while saying that other ways weren't powerful enough to work.

Levi considered Jesus less powerful than him in his early years and more powerful in his later ones, so he was always in this limbo of *more or less* and never in the balance of equal footing. Then all of a sudden Jesus did something that Levi thought was impossible—die and come back—a miracle if ever there was one.

Being a man who lived by the code of authority, Levi wanted that power, too. Naturally, he thought to himself: *What did Jesus do to enable such a miracle? What did he know that I don't? And who knew him well enough to help me?* Plenty of people were only too glad to share what they thought had happened, but you have to live a theory to believe it works and no one could live his theories for him. Levi had a terrible time trying to figure it out. He wanted a reasonable explanation and, for him, that meant the picture explaining the incident, since that's where he thought his own power lived. When Mary suggested he look within to find it, he got uneasy. *Oh no,* he thought, *here comes more of that gobbledygook Jesus was always spouting.* But he secretly feared that even if he did look within, he wouldn't find what he needed.

Maybe he didn't look within because he focused on getting rich.

Money doesn't keep you from looking within; the fear of what you'll find does. But it's no more complicated than noticing your shadow. Whatever it's doing, you're doing, and in the framework of humanness, shadows are found in the people affecting you emotionally. Owning up to those reflections was easy when Levi loved them, but who wants to acknowledge a mirror that's rude, surly, and obnoxious?

Did Mary feel the same about Levi that Joseph did?

She was less tolerant. While she understood how Joseph shared the pain of poverty with Levi, and while she understood how he identified with Levi's need to get out of it and stay out of it, she also understood that Levi took great pleasure in baiting Jesus whenever he could. She was always telling him to solve his problems without involving her son.

Was Jesus doing as much to cause this problem as Levi was?

Yes. Both had to face the truth of their behavior to know why they constantly faced each other. Had Levi believed that looking within could improve his life, he would have tried to do so. He got stuck in thinking that looking within was just another way of getting down on himself or pinpointing flaws. The mirror theory is not one-dimensional. It reflects everything, both what you like about your life and what you don't. The glass doesn't judge what it holds; it's merely a receptacle. How does it taste to you? That's the question. Take responsibility for your content instead of blaming others for what it is. You're the one who knows the taste you enjoy.

When Levi first heard his relatives talking about emotional action/reaction, he thought it sounded easy. Two seconds later an unpleasant mirror showed up and back to blame he went. He listened to the voice who said *you're in this predicament because he did this and she did that* instead of the voice who said *I'm in the predicament because I did this and I did that.* But the whole basis of Jesus' philosophy was that whatever you give, you receive. Not that Jesus didn't have his own lessons in this regard; his were every bit as vivid as Levi's.

Jesus came into the temple on market day in a raging fit and told everyone they better leave or Satan would come in and sweep them all to Hell. Levi, and his associates, through careful negotiation had an arrangement whereby the tradesmen gave the temple a cut of their take in exchange for the use of that space. It worked out well for both parties because few buildings were available and large enough to congregate in and the temple always needed funding. According to their ethics they weren't doing anything wrong. Jesus didn't agree.

He made such a stir that Levi and his associates thought he had gone quite mad. No one wanted to tangle with him so they wound things up and came back later. In Levi's opinion, Jesus had stormed into a scene where lots of happy souls were doing what they loved and having fun in the process. Jesus saw them as transacting with the devil and violating the house of God.

Maybe Jesus was right. Isn't the temple for holy endeavors?
Why isn't business holy?

It just isn't a very spiritual endeavor.
If the people are happy in what they're doing, why is that unspiritual?

It isn't an occupation of high inspirational caliber.
And what do you think is?

Something that helps people—like medicine, priesthood, or charity work.
Does it really matter what people are doing if they're sharing love in the process? Who brings you more cherishing—a merchant who sells you a beautiful dress, or a holy person who lies, cheats, and kicks the poor?

That's an extreme example.
In those times it wasn't, but even if you dislike this analogy, holiness isn't defined by what people are doing; it's defined by the love in their hearts as they do it. Levi wondered why Jesus was so obsessed with his behavior when his own seemed so outrageous. *Oh no,* he thought, *Jesus is at it again, causing a stir, irritating the citizenry, pontificating about morals, and scorning my profession. Why doesn't he stick with what he loves and let me do the same?*

Was that fair?
How would you feel if someone barged into your office and starting yelling and screaming that everyone was going to hell?

I'm sure I'd call security to come and handle the problem.
If Levi and his friends hadn't known Jesus, they would have done the same. A few days later Levi heard that Jesus had a riot at

one of his meetings. He hadn't studied the concept of emotional action/reaction but he wasn't surprised to hear what had happened. Later, when Jesus shared his process, he said that between the moment of accountability and the moment of using that knowledge effectively, a testing period occurs. During that testing period, compassion for self is important. Growth is a gradual process of give/receive one day at a time.

At the temple on market day, Jesus gave judgment with a lot of hot temper around it. Therefore, he received the harsh judgment of others. But he understood that he didn't have to reexperience that harshness if he looked within to understand the reason he faced it. Eventually, he realized that whether he approved of the rabbi's policy or not, he wasn't the one to approve or disapprove. The temple had its own hierarchy for that.

Why did he think he had a right to question that policy?

Why do you think you have a right to question other people's policies?

I guess I get caught up in thinking I'm wiser.

I guess he was caught up in the same dilemma.

I just can't see him as living the same action/reaction as the rest of us.

Why not? He believed in the law of action/reaction so profoundly, he took it to the limit of his imagination. When he did, he found his source. Since he knew that his source was love, he knew that if he loved as deeply as the source loved, he and that source would be one. After achieving this oneness, he wanted to share it. He chose the crucifixion because it was public enough to get a lot of attention. He figured that if people saw with their own eyes that love could conquer even the most hideously perceived of deaths, he could truly make an impression with his philosophy. He came to that state of oneness by believing in himself. He found his core through meditation, listening within instead of without.

Anyone can find what Jesus found in any path or meditation favored. You only have to honor what feels right to you while releasing others to what feels right to them. The force of emotional action/reaction has no look; it has a feeling. Many ways exist to live it. What you deal with isn't important. Finding the love in what you're dealing with is.

I don't think of God as having anything to do with money.

God is the everyone who exists so God has something to do with money on a fairly regular basis. You don't find your way back to autonomy by releasing your need for money. You find your way back by loving the way the Earth runs itself today. A *should be* philosophy is very frustrating. At one time or another, both Jesus and Levi suffered this syndrome. Jesus didn't like it any more than Levi did.

But Levi acted in a way that let Jesus down.

Why would Jesus be let down by Levi's behavior? Jesus needed to have faith in his own behavior instead of worrying about Levi's. Each of them mistrusted the other but neither of them could know the nature of others until they knew their own completely. It wasn't wrong of Jesus to want Levi to change, just futile. Levi lived for his own edification, not Jesus'. Whether or not Jesus understood Levi was irrelevant. Understanding self was the key.

Levi needed to release Jesus and move on. That was hard for him. Probably for the same reason you find it's difficult to forgive the people you think have wronged you. Believe it or not, they are not the bane of your existence; they are the miracle waiting to happen. We all come here to deal with exactly the folks we face, and for exactly the opportunities they offer. The question is: *are you ready to love or aren't you?*

Why should I love a person who caused me pain, Charlie?

Because this is where the miracle is—in the love you discover that otherwise wouldn't exist.

Was business as much of a passion for Levi as spiritual goals were for Jesus?

Business captured his complete and undivided attention just as otherworldly ideas captured Jesus'. And Levi worked every bit as hard to achieve his goals as Jesus worked to achieve his. In this respect, they mirrored each other perfectly. But just because their values were different doesn't mean one was wrong and the other one right. Each of them had their longings to fulfill, each of them knew the path that would help them do it, and each of them found the people with whom to try. When either lost that focus, the process faltered; and at one time or another, it faltered for both of them. One or the other would resort to criticisms or belittling, depending on who was involved and what was at stake.

Levi couldn't forgive Jesus' blatant condemnation and persistent badgering, so he couldn't release. Therefore, he moved on to more opportunities through which to try. Jesus finally realized that his own pursuits couldn't pay off until he released Levi to his. Therefore, he moved on to enlightenment.

> Each day has opportunities to release.
> You either take them and find ease,
> Or you don't, and find dis-ease.

Worksheet for Chapter 3: Levi

When have you judged the choices of others?

When have they judged yours?

Do you love your choices and approve of your decisions?

If not, how can you expect others to honor them?

Take each judge-filled thought and fill it with approval.

Questions to Ponder

• Do I love the path I have chosen or am I telling others the paths they should have chosen?

• Do I rate the jobs around me or do I look beyond the job and value the person living it?

• Do I listen to the voice of compassion or do I listen to the voice of judgment?

> Time is a gift for rediscovering self.
> Put all of your hopes and dreams for love
> Into your own actions
> So all of them can return to abundance.

Personal Insights

Levi's story forced me to face a confusion that began in my childhood. In Sunday school, I heard about a man called Jesus who was poor, but more importantly good and godly. Having a logical mind even then, I deduced that a person who was rich would have to be the opposite—bad and ungodly. I know my reasoning was simplistic, but simplistic or not, millions of people joined me in this belief. By the age of forty, I was still running into quite a few—and unfortunately, I was still confusing wealth with guilt. Sunday school teachers weren't with me anymore, but New Age aficionados were, and all of us saw ourselves as the healers who would free this world of materialism. Levi's story put into words what I have long suspected is true—that the love of money has nothing to do with evil. Evil has to do with disrespecting what you love.

4

James: The Envious Brother

Coveting another's gift
Weakens your own position
By keeping you so focused on
What you think you should have
That what you do have goes unnoticed.

Was James the jealous type?

There is no jealous type, only the type who forgets to love the dream it has. Like everyone else, James came here to cherish his creation—the personification of him in form. Therefore, when he didn't, he wasted his time in a futile focus, often around the personification of Jesus. His brother seemed to have everything James wanted: respect, admiration, opportunity, intellect, wit, and wisdom. So even though James had wonderful qualities that suited his goals, his preoccupation with Jesus made him forgetful—and forgetfulness caused insecurity. In truth, these two had much in common, both of them longing for spiritual attainment. But the fact of their common goal was James' greatest challenge. Had he looked elsewhere for satisfaction, he wouldn't have cared what Jesus accomplished. As the younger brother, never quite holding his own, he suffered by comparison. And for a while, he thought that he couldn't be worthy unless he compared more favorably.

Did James ever side with Levi over Jesus?

When particularly irritated with Jesus, he did. He sided with Levi when Jesus stormed into the temple with threats and accusations. His ties to the rabbi were strong, and he never shared Jesus' compulsion to challenge old tenets in outward and visible ways.

What did Jesus tell James about spiritual attainment?

Whatever he understood at every level of his own. Before he left to travel, he told James to do what he was doing. That didn't sit well with James. He resented being told that his attainment depended on what Jesus was doing to find his. But he wanted what Jesus had without all the hard work Jesus put into getting it. And although he knew he wouldn't be happy doing what Jesus did, he still felt jealous.

That doesn't make any sense.

Jealousy never does.

Did James and Jesus spend a lot of time together?

That depended on what they were after at any given moment. As Jesus approached puberty, his passion was information and since most of what he wanted to know was inside the temple, he spent whatever time he could spare there. James often tagged along because the temple offered an atmosphere of spiritual history he enjoyed. The fact that Jesus left him alone to explore its nooks and crannies made it even more appealing. If James got bored, he'd ask Jesus what he was reading. Jesus would tell him and ask if he wanted to read it, too. Poring over lengthy tomes was not his idea of fun. When he asked Jesus what he was learning, Jesus said he was trying to understand what those before him had known. When James asked him what that was, he said he didn't know yet, but as soon as he did he'd let him know.

Although James could be a pest at times, Jesus usually welcomed him. The reading got tedious now and then. When Jesus needed a break, he'd ask James what he thought of a certain idea. Often he liked his answers better than the ones he read since James' were honest and simple.

Pest or not, though, James accompanied Jesus as often as possible, enjoying the freedom it gave him away from the house. Mary gave birth with astounding regularity, which made James uncomfortable. Not only because of the time Mary spent with the babies but also because of the extra duties it gave to him. He tried his best to escape them, not always successfully but always with determined effort, and eventually he was called the master of excuses. Even more grating than the fact of the babies was the fact that his mother always seemed to have time for them and never enough for him.

Not wanting to hear how incorrigible he was, he often disappeared with his older brother when Jesus headed for the temple. If his mother caught him before he was out the door, she gave him a good tongue-lashing. If she didn't catch him, she consoled herself with the fact that at least he was off with Jesus instead of the mischief-makers he called his friends.

What James couldn't see in those days was that his needs would have been handled had he helped Mary handle hers. He wanted the same tender devotion she gave to the little ones whether he'd helped her out or not. And, maddeningly, she never seemed to mind when Jesus took off in the middle of chaos. What he didn't acknowledge was how often Jesus stopped what he was doing to be of service. So in her mind Jesus had earned the right to leave while James had not. Perhaps had he felt more guilty about his behavior, he would have been motivated to change it. But he never thought about guilt in the middle of chaos, only afterward.

Did Mary and Joseph have favorites?

James thought so, especially when he didn't get what he wanted.

Hurt feelings are legitimate when parents have favorites.

All feelings are legitimate regardless of why you have them but James' dilemma had nothing to do with Mary and Joseph. He lived the result of his own emotional enactment, not theirs. As he gave, he received, regardless of what his parents were doing.

Infants can't make decisions to include or exclude but many times they suffer rejection.

They may be rejected but they won't suffer from it if they haven't caused suffering for others.

Are you referring to what may have been lived in a past lifetime, Charlie?

In terms of the soul's growth, lifetimes are meaningless. The soul lives what it needs whenever it has a chance to. If the soul comes into humanness to live rejection in infancy, it's looking for information, not suffering. The body may be young but the soul is eternally wise. If a child is rejected but has no need to feel rejection, that child will be oblivious to anything but the love and nourishment it does need to feel.

When James felt rejected by Jesus, that feeling had nothing to do with Jesus' behavior; it had to do with his behavior. This is everyone's challenge: to remember that life creates from the inside out, not the outside in.

Was James around when Jesus returned from traveling?

Yes, he was around. His homecoming caused quite a stir. People started praising Jesus left and right for striking out on his own. All of a sudden his rival was back, getting all the attention again. Hoping to diminish Jesus' importance and enhance his own, he withdrew from the house as if to prove that he was too busy with his life to bother with Jesus. James did notice, however, that Jesus was very different from the man he remembered.

Before he left, Jesus was vocal and often impatient. Now he was soft-spoken and relaxed. But regardless of how Jesus had changed or what that meant to his progress, resentment on James' part deterred his progress. As far as he was concerned, he was again taking second place as the not-quite spiritual son. He wanted recognition, too, but he certainly had no intention of doing what Jesus had done to find his.

Most of the time, jealousy was a fleeting emotion. It only interfered when allowed to eat at his soul for hours on end, causing neglect of his own inspired interests—one of them being the joy of music. He played an instrument somewhat like a fiddle and although he wasn't proficient, he was better than anyone else in the family and that was good enough for him.

Many times, while amusing the family with lilting tunes, he faced the difficult task of relinquishing the spotlight to Jesus. The only instrument Jesus played was his vocal cords, but he sure knew how to play them to get attention. He graciously conceded the spotlight to James, but the second James stopped, Jesus would start again.

Consistent to the bone, James handled his musical attainment the way he handled his spiritual attainment, wanting immediate results or giving up. He hadn't yet learned that true achievement came from focus with lots of persistence backing it up. In fact, he didn't stick with anything long enough to call it a career until Jesus came back from his travels. Then he enlisted in the militia.

It wasn't a popular choice in the household and given his parent's priorities, unexpected. But it seemed like a good way of saying that he could strike out on his own, too. As a part of this hired militia, his job was to settle skirmishes in outlying provinces and minimize the conflicts. At least he thought that was his job. He wanted to be of service and so believed what he heard. It seemed to him that a lot of service was needed in this harsh uncaring society. Naiveté extended way beyond the job description because he thought helping others was about changing their lives, not changing his.

When he took this job, Jesus didn't offer opinions and James didn't ask for any but he did hope for approval. After all, Jesus had been a rebel, too. Much had happened to both of them in the interim, however. Jesus had gone from being a skeptic with little faith in his own choices to a believer with lots of faith in James'. James had gone from a younger brother trying to emulate an older brother to a sour teenager trying to find a pursuit worthy of his arrogance. Later, when Jesus came back from his self-imposed isolation, his growth was more dramatic. When James asked him how he'd found such bliss, Jesus said he'd gone to the source—his own tender heart—and if James wanted to find the same growth, he only had to go to the tenderness in his.

What a surprise, James thought, *having my own wisdom praised,* something he wasn't used to. Not that Jesus hadn't tried to help him before, he had. But James wanted answers that appealed to him, not those telling him to read volumes of information, travel halfway around the world, and go off and live by himself. *Tell me my way* is what he said to Jesus. *What do I need to do? Where do I need to go? Whom do I need to find?* Jesus never had those answers and they were the only ones James wanted. That's why Jesus' new response was so appealing. It meant that James didn't have to do anything except share his heart in whatever way felt comfortable.

Did Jesus know what James needed and just withhold that information?

Do you know what others need for living more meaningful lives?

I sometimes think so.

Well Jesus often thought so, too, but the more he thought he had those answers, the more James resisted what he said they were.

When James enlisted in the militia, was it for philanthropic reasons or to get himself noticed.

Both, since he chose to be philanthropic—or what he told himself at the time was philanthropic—in a way that got him noticed. And rather than look too closely at what he was getting into, he convinced himself that this was the step he needed: a chance to be of service to others; a chance to have more fun in life; a chance to make a living; a chance to look sophisticated to the women he wanted to impress. And most of all, a chance to do the unexpected and find reward.

Things didn't go well. Then he beat himself up for choosing badly, and along with personal regret came a voice insisting that Jesus never made mistakes. In an effort to feel better, James diminished Jesus in any way he could—devaluing his love and emphasizing his shortcomings in hopes that people would lose faith in Jesus and gain faith in him. It didn't work. Instead he got the backstabbing of others when he least expected it. When his family asked him how he liked his job, he pretended enthusiasm. He certainly wasn't about to listen to a lot of *I told you so's*.

With expectations so high, James wasn't happy when the job got him the cruelty of others and plenty of self-loathing. Even the income was hard to enjoy as relatives scorned him for how he was earning it. But he was a person with lots of dreams and very little discipline to back them up. Working in the militia had valuable lessons for a big talker with minimum follow-through. It also showed him what he *didn't* want to be disciplined about and that was helpful, too.

In the end, he felt betrayed. He thought he'd been hired as a peacemaker not an aggressor. Instead, he had to cope with minor rebellions, whatever the cost in lives. Having a job where the primary purpose was to spy on and threaten others was loathsome to him. He wanted to escape but a term of service was required and the militia didn't take kindly to shirkers.

James was forced to understand discipline even if the process was painful, but if the conscious mind refuses to live growth comfortably, the soul resorts to living it uncomfortably.

What does that mean, Charlie?
It means that the soul has vision that often the conscious mind does not. When the conscious you refuses to face timely growth, the soul forces you to live it anyway. You may see it as suffering; the soul sees it as destiny.

Can you give me an example?

Sure. Use James. He put himself in a situation where it was almost impossible not to find more discipline. His soul knew that more of it had to be found—one way or another—because his emotional goals were being thwarted until he did. While living that pain, James was too depressed to believe that anything good could result from suppressing the helpless. Later, he was able to see the value in what he had learned.

How did James learn to play music if he was lacking in discipline?

Music was a way of getting attention. As he got it, his skills improved. No one pushed him to excel and even had they, it wouldn't have mattered. He needed to honor his talent with time, effort, and patience. His inability to follow-through was a familiar pattern to those who knew him. Most had to deal with it one way or another. His attitude was *Oh well, if this doesn't work out, I'll charm myself into something else.*

He was an attractive, intelligent, and engaging youngster who found that with a little extra coaxing and cajoling, anything he wanted could be his. Since the goal was always to get attention, regardless of the means, the goal was always reached. Thinking that outer influences were the source of his satisfaction, he never stuck to inner disciplines long enough to understand their reward. He could have found it in the study of music if his goal had been to master the instrument. He played for attention. Therefore, when attention arrived, the instrument lost importance.

Would a different focus have helped him?

A different focus eventually did. Had he not lived the ones that came before it, he wouldn't have welcomed the one that worked. Even the art of concentration is a step-by-step mastery. For instance, what would you do if you wanted to play a harp?

I'd buy one, and then I'd find a teacher who knew how to play one.

That's a good beginning. You're bound to learn something from the person who knows that mastery. Then what?

I'd work on learning a few notes and hopefully some tunes.

After you mastered the easy ones, you'd have a foundation on which to build. James thought he could go from need to mastery without anything in between. Jesus understood the process. James didn't believe in the worthiness of the moment. Therefore, he was always moving on to something else that might prove worthy. Before any future endeavors could feel important, he had to value himself in whatever he was doing.

Did James see himself as undeserving?

Sometimes, but that was also his belief to deal with. To change it, he had to take responsibility for owning it in the first place. Instead, he blamed others when life seemed meaningless. He heard himself saying over and over, *I could have tried harder, but why bother? Life will disappoint me anyway.* Had he at least taken responsibility for being so negative he would have lessened the pain he felt, and that would have lessened the pain he attracted back.

Did Jesus' achievements have a negative effect on James?

When he spent all his time focusing on Jesus, they did. James had wonderful qualities, too: a delightful musicality, a vital athleticism, and a courtly way with the women. Many times Jesus watched him with longing in his heart. But he never let that focus persist. He was more interested in honoring what he did well, concentrating on the source of joy instead of the source of misery.

Granted, some people have more determination than others but only because they've developed that skill. James got more of it as he realized that no other person could give it to him no matter how many years he lived, how many experiences he had, or how many people he encountered.

Later, when he looked back over his life, he saw how he'd lived the first half of it as a person trying to win the race to prove himself a winner. In the second half he'd realized that winners were those in love with the race. Awakening came as he saw how appreciation for the game had enabled Jesus to rise above his Earthly limitations.

Jesus had known the reason he'd entered the fray in the first place—love for the contender. His resurrection was pivotal to James. It helped him to understand how he'd gotten off track. Jesus did not believe that others knew better than he did what he should do with his life. Therefore, he believed in his choices. James had no faith in his.

After the resurrection James decided that if Jesus had lived his miracles, he could live some, too. But first, he had to honor his pleasures the way that Jesus had honored his. Not everyone is musical or athletic, nor is everyone a great orator like Jesus, but each soul has a truth it came here to live and only that soul can expand it.

It may seem to you that some people are more gifted than others, but gifts are chosen for the wisdom they offer the soul. Talent for talent, James had many more than Jesus. How many you have is not what makes or breaks your journey. How you deal with the ones you have is. After James found discipline he found more pleasure. Not that people hadn't pleased him before. They had, but this feeling went deeper. It revealed the source, which meant that he could find it again without depending on anyone else to get it.

After the military James lived his own new beginning just as Jesus had gone on to live his and took up reform within the temple. His hope was to rekindle some of the love that Jesus had hoped to inspire. Although Jesus had not succeeded, the field was left more fertile because of his efforts. Reform hadn't played well to Jesus' strengths; it played well to James'. Jesus found it difficult to be tactful and diplomatic. James found it easy. Jesus found it difficult to stay in one location for very long. James found it easy. Jesus found it difficult to compromise. James found it easy.

Take stock of your life. You have what it takes if you're willing to notice your attributes and how they suit your goals. When James saw Jesus again—alive and well after the resurrection—he knew that Jesus hadn't left. He was around and always would be, looking for ways to help others find wholeness. Therefore James didn't think of his awakening as something that happened after Jesus had gone, but as something that finally allowed the two of them to work together in harmony.

The miracles around Jesus always got James' attention, but the ones he lived were the true creators. As soon as he went from blaming others for everything wrong in his life to taking responsibility for his emotional actions, he and Jesus were together in terms of emotion. Their mutual friends were a great help, too, gathering people together to discuss problems, reflect on goals, and find solutions. James disciplined himself to attend these sessions and gained enormous insight.

Gradually, he began to realize that Jesus had known for a long time what he was just beginning to realize, that help didn't necessarily come from those he thought should be giving it. But if he kept his heart open, he'd feel that help wherever it was.

Didn't Jesus' friends become wise as a result of knowing him?
No, they became wise from knowing themselves.

Would you say that James had a difficult path?
When he predicted doom and gloom, he did. When he predicted joy and happiness, he found that premise instead. To his credit, he eventually realized how envy had poisoned his experience. His worst moments came when he saw himself as partly responsible for Jesus' fate. Opportunities arose to support him and he did not. Fear controlled him. Fear that he'd be seen in the same undesirable light as Jesus. Fear also convinced him that his fate hinged on what others decided to do, not on what he decided to do. That's why he thought Jesus' fate had hinged on what he had done, not on what Jesus had done. Happily, guilt didn't last. When he saw Jesus alive and well after the resurrection, he felt the power inside himself as he felt the power in Jesus. And what a change in attitude! Before the resurrection, he saw Jesus as powerless to fulfill his prophecy.

When Jesus returned three days later, James was thrilled to let him take the spotlight. By then he knew that a constant focus on Jesus and his achievements had kept him from honoring his. After the military, he worked within the temple, his lifelong dream. Although he struggled at first, the constant reminder of Jesus' resurrection and their ensuing reunion helped him to focus on his hopes and dreams. Eventually he realized that excellence wasn't about how well he did something; it was about how well he felt in the doing. As soon as he started loving the process, he started loving the continuity.

That's beautiful, Charlie.

Most things are that put an emphasis on self-respect. We live our beliefs, helpful or not, so it's wise to stay aware of what they are. Jesus saw himself, and everyone else in the family, as a valuable part of the whole to which all belonged and contributed. James did not. Jesus respected the right to be different while honoring the individuality of others. James did not. Jesus embraced a philosophy encouraging self-esteem, while at the same time, demonstrating why it was wise to do so. James did not.

Jesus believed that a person's attitude was the difference between a delightful journey and one that was filled with envy, fear, and acrimony. James did not. Jesus could look at his shortcomings and have a good laugh. James could not. Jesus could forget about his failures and remember his successes. James could not. Jesus could ignore the people who didn't believe in him and attend the people who did. James could not. Until Jesus showed James through the resurrection that it was possible to become the everything he believed in, James was the everything he did not.

> Jealousy gains a foothold
> When you lose a grip on
> The only solid footing you have—
> Your own tender expression.

Worksheet for Chapter 4: James

Of whom do you feel a certain amount of jealousy?

What does that person have that you want?

If you got it, would you really know how to use it?

Which is more important to you: having what you really need or having what you think you want?

List all the good reasons for what you already have.

Questions to Ponder

• Am I interested in who I am or am I interested in who everyone else is?

• Am I listening to the well of wisdom within or doubting my instincts every step of the way?

• When time runs out, will I be happy I had this journey or will I be sorry for how I used my time?

> Wisdom has many faces in many places
> But only in order to love its many graces.

Personal Insights

I had a lot of thinking to do after hearing James' story. It forced me to examine the envious feelings I've had—and there were plenty of them—especially in terms of one particular person. As far as I was concerned, she had everything I wanted: recognition in her field, respect for her ideas, and money to reaffirm that her talent was seen as worthy. I had never experienced such awful feelings to the extent that I did then. To make matters worse, guilt was in the mix because she had assisted me enormously at a crucial time in my life. How could I entertain such emotion when she had been so willing to serve in any way she could? Truthfully, the only thing that healed me was time: time to expand my talent, time to appreciate my uniqueness, and time to understand that the help I needed had been there for me exactly when I needed it.

5

Simon:
The Hero-Worshipping Brother

If you want to live
Another's defined beauty,
Make sure that definition
Appeals to you.

Is that what Simon did, live another's defined beauty?

It's what he tried to do. His goal was simple: to stay in pure and loving thought. And since Jesus wanted the same, Simon thought he should take his cue from him. But Simon had instincts, too. Sometimes they jibed with Jesus', sometimes not. When they didn't, Simon wondered if something was wrong with his. He hadn't yet learned that happiness came from honoring his ideals, not copying another's.

Why did he have this problem?

He suffered from being the third son. He was also a twin to his brother, Joses. He found it easy to dominate Joses with a flashier personality and a bigger body, but he didn't find it easy to cope with James. And James wasn't so happy to be faced with yet another competitor in Simon. Later, when Simon aligned himself with Jesus, James felt even more threatened. Driven by this fear, he minimized Simon's importance every chance he got.

Did Simon have any envy of Jesus?

No, he was adoring of Jesus and wanted to be exactly like him. But whether you envy or idolize, you diminish yourself. Simon had the same lesson of learning to appreciate himself that James had.

Was Jesus comfortable with Simon copying him?

Before he returned from traveling, he was. He wanted that affirmation. He thought it confirmed his position and the rightness of his opinions.

Was Jesus happy in his philosophy?

Later in life he was. In his youth, his views were often erratic. He wasn't convinced that happiness was the goal anyway; righteousness had more play. When righteousness brought him a lot of pain, he started to reevaluate. *How can something be worthy if it makes me feel so miserable?* After careful deliberation, he decided that a broader itinerary might bring him the views he preferred. After discovering where to look for them, he succeeded.

Did Jesus have enough in the world to make him happy?

He had enough in the world to satisfy his particular longings but *things* couldn't make him happy regardless of what they numbered. Things are illusory. Illusion can't hold emotion. He had to love the things he had in order to find contentment. When he didn't, dissatisfaction grew.

Jesus was no more immune to this kind of drama than anyone. He had to take responsibility for his emotions and figure out why he had them. As he opened his heart to answers, he seeded his power to re-create. Early success made him quite optimistic about the future.

Simon, in contrast, couldn't get past the influence of others. His blind support of Jesus and the criticism he gave to those who didn't support him attracted negative thinkers. Then negative thinkers did their best to intimidate him. He wanted to shed this negative influence and have a healthy outlook, but the constant criticism he gave brought constant criticizers back.

Isn't it helpful now and then to be critical?
If you put flowers in a trashcan, does it remain a trashcan?

On the outside it does but the inside doesn't smell like one.
Well, Simon stayed the same on the outside, too. Inside, where feelings are, he was the content he put there. If he filled that space with approval, he had a receptacle filled with the same. If he didn't, he had whatever he put there instead.

Irritated by his own vulnerability he resorted to rigidity, hoping that a carefully controlled environment would keep him focused wisely. It didn't. Rigidity made it difficult to release any previously held positions that no longer served his path.

Jesus was rigid too, but to Jesus, rigidity meant loving his truth regardless of who else shared it. To Simon it meant insisting on *one* truth. The older Jesus got, the more he knew how to use his rigid stubbornness in a productive way. It manifested in his ability to hold onto his faith in the face of many doubters. Simon admired his usage, for he stayed rigid out of fear.

Did Simon see Jesus as a rebel?
Yes, quite often and he was, not only when it came to personal

growth but social reform as well. He mocked the temple for its out-dated policies and the government for its cruel ones. Simon was fond of Jesus. In his effort to emulate him, he mimicked his way of doing things—acting as he acted, looking as he looked, talking as he talked, praying as he prayed, blessing as he blessed, and befriending as he befriended. Everyone needs a role model at times. But when Simon needed one, he adopted the behavior he saw instead of the principles he loved. Then, anyone not behaving as Jesus behaved was suspect.

Critical assessment didn't win him fans; it won him the oppo-site. After many painful mirrors, he decided he'd rather be with those who had the *wrong beliefs* and were happy than with those who had the *right beliefs* and weren't.

Did Jesus show any favoritism to Simon because he was his brother?

No. Simon wished he would, sure that his life would improve if Jesus did. Simon was mistaken. His life improved when he paid more attention to what he needed. Jesus had answers that he believed in. Simon assumed they were right for everyone. But the soul who insists on right versus wrong, good versus bad, and acceptable versus unacceptable doesn't want to get caught in the lesser side of these equations.

In awe of Jesus off and on for most of his life, Simon got con-fused. When awe told him that Jesus was wonderful because he was special, his belief was self-destructive. When awe told him that Jesus was wonderful because he loved so deeply, his belief was helpful. The former said that he couldn't find the same love Jesus had. The latter said that the same love could be his if he went deep enough to enjoy it. When the former got a hold of him, he thought to himself *I can't be this and I can't be that because I'm lesser. I can't do this and I can't do that because I'm weaker. I can't know this and I can't know that because I'm denser.*

Jesus was older, but he never flaunted age as a reason for wis-dom. Simon's love for Jesus was total when his love for himself was total. When Simon was young and inexperienced, bonding was easy. As he matured, he couldn't see past Jesus' way of doing things to find his way of doing things. Hero-worship prevented him from sensing any deeper into his own potential.

A feisty temperament pushed him to argue for the sake of argument, provoke for the sake of debate, and exaggerate for the sake of expression, anything to get his body into motion and his mind into gear. Honoring this side of his nature was easy when Jesus shared it, and before Jesus left to travel he did. He told people what to do, when to do it, and how to do it. Later, when Jesus returned from solitude, he was more like a lamb than a lion and Simon was still a stallion.

This was confusing to Simon. Instead of telling people how to live and what to do, Jesus was telling people to trust their instincts and follow their hearts. Simon didn't know what to make of this new Jesus or how to fit his own personality into the mix. The more he tried to emulate Jesus, the more inadequate he felt. And it didn't help that James was constantly scorning him for his apery.

Family and friends reminded Simon that Jesus hadn't always been so levelheaded and mature but that didn't help. He admired the lamb in Jesus. He just didn't realize that the lamb was happy because it was honoring itself as a lamb in the moment. Desperate to be more like him, Simon ignored the stallion within and tried to be what he wasn't. He reasoned that if the lamb were Jesus, the stallion was the devil and had to be purged. Thankfully, you can't find happiness in denial. Otherwise his answer would have been to know Jesus through and through instead of himself through and through, and I can't imagine a more frustrating pursuit.

Didn't Jesus say we should love ourselves?

Yes. Love who you are, honor everyone else, and give what you hope to receive.

He lived differently than most people do.

That's the very thought that kept Simon so off balance. In truth he didn't. Jesus lived whatever made him happy.

Other people haven't found what he found.

Oh, but they have, some before Jesus, some during his life-time, and many after he left. The fulfillment of those before him convinced Jesus of his own potential.

When Simon tried to honor himself, he heard debating voices inside his head. One voice said *Jesus is the reason you live. Jesus has all the answers. Jesus knows what is right and anyone disagreeing with him is doomed to hell forever.* The other voice said *Jesus keeps you stag-nant, Jesus keeps you stupid, Jesus keeps you dependent.* Neither was accurate. But he swung back and forth, listening to one and then the other, searching for a truth that worked for him. His faulty thinking began from believing that he could only achieve what Jesus had achieved if their lives were running parallel. Therefore, when they didn't, he panicked. And it didn't take much to upset Simon, since all of his hopes for happiness were pinned on the actions of Jesus.

Simon's first challenge came when Jesus decided to travel. He didn't want him to go; sure that he'd miss him terribly. Happily, other friendships came along and life went on as usual. The sec-ond challenge came when Jesus said he was leaving again, this time for solitude. Hating his decision, Simon tried to change his mind. *I'll be miserable if you leave,* he told him. Jesus said he couldn't find his heart's desire by making Simon happy; for that he had to rely on himself. Then Simon laughed because he hadn't even con-sidered Jesus' happiness.

Years later, when Jesus returned from solitude, the govern-ment wanted someone to blame for the escalating conflicts. Fearing that Jesus would take the blame, Simon begged him to stop his preaching. Jesus said that preaching brought him pleas-ure and pleasure was the safety he sought. Family and friends did all that they could to change his mind, but Jesus had nothing to fear. He'd given up fear by understanding where it came from. And since it came from the fear he'd given to others and he hadn't given any, he had no reason to expect it back.

Did Jesus think a martyred death would turn him into a hero?

Jesus thought death impossible and therefore martyrdom irrelevant. Simon couldn't relate to such faith. How could Jesus stay fearless in the face of pain and agony? It made no sense to him. And the talk of pain was just the beginning. How could he ignore everyone's efforts to save him? How could he be so stupid, so naive, and so dense? How could he be so sure of his rightness when everyone else thought him wrong?

Did Jesus speak of dying to save us from our sins?

Jesus didn't believe in sins, dying, or saving. He referred to sins as the mind of God in confusion—or the mind forgetting to serve the soul within. To him eternal life was a given; therefore death impossible. In terms of saving, Jesus knew that he couldn't save anyone because no one had been able to save him. He'd had to save himself. Therefore, he wanted everyone—even those who considered themselves his enemy—to witness his transformation.

He demonstrated that a mind full of love is a body full of love. Granted, it's hard to believe in a feat that hasn't yet proven possible to you, but you live beliefs today that eluded you in the past. You know they work because you live them every day. Once an idea is lived, it's yours. The natural process of growth is to test what might be achievable. Every effort you make is redefining that purpose.

Did Simon have a job where decision-making was important?

We all have this job. Energy lives to create and expand. Therefore, the more Simon honored his life, the happier he got. Decisions, per se, are not as important as how you behave while making them. Simon entered most transactions suspiciously, expecting to catch a thief, but at least he wasn't surprised when he did. Before he saw how belligerence attracted its mirror, he spread a lot of belligerence around. After he saw how civility attracted its mirror, he adopted a different viewpoint.

Simon knew that a deal wasn't viable if only one of the dealers benefited. But the truth is people didn't care; they only wanted the best for themselves. To live comfortably, Simon had to keep his goal in the forefront of mind. If the energy around him depleted that effort, he was better off without it anyway.

That's a comforting thought.

The study of oneness always is. To understand any lack in your life, ask the following questions: *Where do I feel denied? Where do I feel unsupported? Where do I feel needy?* This is the guidance you need for turning things around. Give to get your heart's desire. This is how creation begins, this is how creation expands, and this is how you re-create to begin again.

Did Simon's family compare him to Jesus?

Not only to Jesus, they compared all of the brothers to one another, not maliciously but in hopes of seeing them develop into strong masterful adults. It was rarely done tactfully. Intentions were admirable, to raise healthy and disciplined contributing members of society. Healthy development, however, rarely comes out of negative judgment; it comes out of positive praise. Consequently, all of them felt ever challenged to believe in themselves and ever thwarted to respect each other.

Were James and Simon good friends?

At times; James was a maverick in terms of companionship, and Simon often detested the friends he chose. As a devoted disciple, looking for truth under Jesus' guidance, Simon angered James. And James, being jealous of Jesus, formed his own group of disciples. When Simon preferred Jesus' group, James taunted him, calling him Jesus' slave.

Did James really dislike Jesus?

There were times when he thought he did. James played second fiddle to Jesus an awful lot of the time. After Jesus was no longer present, James came into his own. The revelations that followed inspired a leadership in James that allowed many of Jesus' ideas to spread and find a bigger audience.

After Jesus left, did Simon and James continue to feud?

Their relationship went from enmity to tolerance as James gained his own reputation and Simon learned to control his temper. They were never best friends, but they matured and accepted each other within the family unit.

Did their feuding upset Mary and Joseph?

To Joseph it seemed like typical male behavior: two strong contenders vying for supremacy. To Mary, it was troublesome. She didn't like that one brother pitted himself against another in a hateful way. But she did accept that sibling rivalry existed and she did accept that she'd have to make the best of it. Joseph assured her that the rivalry would lessen over time. She hoped he was right.

Was he?

To the extent that both gained a focus that pleased them.

Did Simon eventually know himself well?

He grew to. His eagerness to be in the "right" idea with the right person at the right time caused rigidity when flexibility was called for. His natural tendency to be dramatic caused flamboyancy when composure was called for. Add to that the constant nagging he got to behave more appropriately and he found himself in a quandary. How to support the healer he saw Jesus becoming while still respecting himself? As he pushed for others to be more like Jesus, a method of coping he'd learned from his elders, his own uniqueness suffered. Life only improved when he realized that before he could fully appreciate the man he hoped to be, he had to appreciate the man he already was.

> Live what you believe in.
> Give what you hope to receive.
> All that you need
> Is found from these two directives.

Worksheet for Chapter 5: Simon

What behavior have you copied in the past year?

What did you hope to gain from doing so?

What did you get that you least expected?

What did you get that you most expected?

Would you use this method again to accomplish a goal, and if not, what method would you use?

Questions to Ponder

- Do I value my individuality or do I use it as a weapon to separate from others?

- If I push others to love, will I end up with love or will I end up with pushiness?

- As I plan for the future, do I ask how much I'll get or do I ask how much I'll give?

   The wisdom within doesn't need outer agreement.
   It needs inner cooperation.

Personal Insights

   After hearing Simon's story, I thought to myself: I remember what it's like to feel that I'm not the person I should be. I remember what it's like to feel belittled for my beliefs, for the rituals I find helpful, and for the people I find informative. I remember what it's like to be told my goals are less important, my pleasures less informative, and my politics less relevant. And I remember . . . Wait a minute! I also remember what it's like to wish that others were different. Oops! Sorry, you all, if you're one of those people. If it's any consolation, neither position was enjoyable. Simon's story reminded me that I only had to be the person I wanted to be to face the same deliverance in others.

6

Mariah: The Reflective Sister

Every detail is meaningful,
And symbolizes
How you're living your life.

Was Mariah the sister closest to Jesus in age?

She was. Her name was Mary, named after her mother. For clarity, I'm calling her Mariah.

Was she close to Jesus emotionally?

They got along well. He symbolized all that she admired in a man: approachable demeanor, a lack of arrogance, and a willingness to look for the good in others. In that respect, Mariah had her mirror.

Is that what you mean by details being symbolic?

Sure. She had details reflecting the kind of person she was; even in things concerning matter. Her home told her about her leisure habits, her food told her about her eating habits, her clothes told her about her dressing habits, and her emotional habits reflected details as well. Life fluctuates as different priorities inspire different details.

Some things never change, Charlie. For instance, I go to market and buy the same food over and over.

The need for nourishment is a constant. The food you buy is not.

But the food I buy always looks the same.

So might you on the outside. Inside, you are the feelings you put there.

Was Mariah interested in food?

Very much so. Her mother, Mary, a magnificent cook, urged her to use her recipes and expand on them through her own creativity. Mariah did and her skills accelerated. After she married, she used her gift to nourish her family. As her skills improved and the food became delectable, friends dropped by to enjoy the feasts. At first, Mariah thought *how wonderful, my skills are being appreciated.* Happy anticipation soon turned into dreaded drudgery as twice the shopping, twice the spending, and twice the cleanup turned her into a shrew.

Uncomfortable, she cooked stew over and over to reflect her mood. When that didn't help, she hinted for the guests to help her out now and then, and a few of them did. The prevailing mood, however, was that Mariah had a talent to share whether she wanted to or not. Unconcerned for her comfort, people showed up at all hours of the day and evening, forcing her to drop whatever she was doing to accommodate their enthusiasm. It was very annoying. Mariah wanted to share, but she didn't want to sacrifice her peace of mind in the process.

When the problem escalated she turned to Jesus, hoping he'd have a solution. He had several: Serve at certain hours, encourage mutual gifts of nourishment, and never overextend yourself. Liking his advice she told the worst offenders what he suggested. But would you believe it, they all thought she was kidding—especially her brothers. Besides not wanting to hear any proposal that could end their eating pleasures, they weren't convinced she was serious.

When Mariah told Jesus his ideas hadn't worked, he said she hadn't used them. Words and good intentions would only bring her more of the same. To see some action, she had to take some action. She meant to, but the very first time she tried to follow through, she got confronted. Then she lost her nerve and reverted back to habit.

As her joy in the gift diminished, the power to bring it back disappeared. Mariah hoped that treating people to meal after meal would be seen as a loving gesture, but God saw it as the feeling she brought to the process. To infuse more love, she had to stop feeding the stragglers and turn away the users. Jesus used an analogy to help her understand her predicament.

If our grocer is not compensated for his goods, is that a loving situation? No, she said, *but he is in business.* Jesus said, *So what? His gift is that of a grocer. Yours is that of a cook. Why would the universe see them differently? Action/reaction is an emotional force. Just because the grocer's gift has a specific meaning in our particular culture doesn't change the nature of action/reaction. You act; you are acted upon. Put some action behind your intentions and those who want to receive will start to give. Those who don't will understand the terms and act accordingly.*

Not everyone was gracious as Mariah lived this growth, but the behavior of others was not the challenge; her behavior was. Jesus did say, however, that good intentions counted for something because her heart would open to the good intentions of others.

Those who left still cared about Mariah didn't they?

They did and caring was lovely, but it didn't buy the food, set the table, or clean the dishes.

Didn't Mariah want her friends to enjoy the food?

She did, but their enjoyment hadn't gotten her what she needed. *How can I be so cruel as to turn these people away from the food that means so much to them?* She didn't want to be selfish. She wanted to be kind, but she first had to learn the nature of kindness. She thought it meant giving her friends what they loved in the picture, when it truth, it meant showing them someone who loved herself. When she put this premise to work, life improved immediately.

Nothing good ever resulted from denying herself the pleasure of hard-earned reward. She had to respect her place in the circle of human support. For instance, had Mary said to Mariah *here is the stove, here is a pot, here is the food—now cook,* would that be a loving gesture? Well, God is no less loving than she. Wholeness isn't found from living in frustrated angry feelings; it's found from keeping your emotions full and always appreciative. Happily, once she honored her gift, others were ready to honor it, too.

How can I trust this premise, Charlie?

Why do you respect Jesus so much?

Because he loves so easily.

How do you think he got to the point where he could?

By being selfless?

He tried being selfless. Not only did he make himself miserable, he made everyone around him miserable as well. When he tried being selfish, his mood improved immediately. He met resistance, though, just as Mariah did. Plenty of associates preferred the sacrificing Jesus. Nevertheless, he pursued his dreams regardless of who opposed him—parents, siblings, cousins, religion, or friends. Each time he succumbed to the role of martyr, depression set in.

The Jesus who lived in selflessness was not an appealing persona. People avoided him at all costs when he sank into it. Denial was so unpleasant because it pushed him to believe that someone other than himself was responsible for his happiness.

Did Mariah think of Jesus as an intense person?

She thought of him as a deep-feeling soul. His downward-spiraling moods were every bit as intense as his upward-spiraling ones. Jesus struggled as much as anyone to know the God within. He always made an effort to be a good person but his idea of good evolved. As it did, he went through radical changes. Some of them brought harsh reactions from others. That doesn't mean he didn't have love in his heart, he did—even in denial. How could a soul be without love? Love is all there is, but the mind can choose to ignore it.

Jesus gave what he understood at every level of awareness. The more he pleased himself, the more of himself he had to share with others. He found his answers from living what didn't work, figuring out why, and choosing differently. Mariah finally realized that to enjoy her gift, she had to enjoy the gifts of others. To make sure she did, she asked her guests to bring a gift of their own. In fact, she forced them to come up with one by saying *either find a way to contribute, or leave.* Confronting though it was, it was a lot less painful than martyrdom.

When Mariah first started sharing the meals, she told her guests how to reciprocate. Then they told her how to cook. Enough of that, she thought, and stopped with all the prattle. As she encouraged participation, the game of mutual support gradually took on such proportions that a food cooperative evolved. As her heart took up the challenge and the interest of others grew, so did her menu of excellent cuisine. Success didn't come from being selfless, however. It came from remembering that everyone is looking for fulfillment. Therefore anyone living it is an immediate magnet.

It doesn't matter how a person contributes. God doesn't separate gifts into categories, e.g., the gift of tailoring, the gift of carpentry, the gift of cuisine. God sees every part of the whole as having a mutually supportive gift. Even a few kind words can qualify, but the feeling is what creates, not the words. Principles have to work everywhere energy exists, even where words are not. Otherwise, they are useless to the whole.

What alternatives could Mariah have tried in her struggle to self-respect?

She could have let others eat her out of house and home and become a martyr. She could have barred outsiders and become a recluse. She could have demanded money for the hiring of a maid and the buying of food, and become a tyrant. These alternatives had no appeal.

Couldn't she have trusted that whatever she gave would come back?

This is what happened. Action/reaction prevailed whether she trusted physics or not. The universe honors every expression as worthy—even if only to demonstrate the nature of discontent—which is what happened to Mariah. She lived in martyrdom and the gift of martyrdom returned.

Martyrdom is not a gift, Charlie.

The universe doesn't judge your offering, Betsy. It assumes you want whatever you give. That's why it behooves you to know exactly what you *are* giving.

There's something missing here. God gives unconditionally. If we want to be this force, we have to do the same.

God gives unconditionally whatever is given. Therefore, frustration, confusion, and denial came back to her with no conditions whatsoever. The pure heart of God is not a selfless energy; it's an energy that knows the love of the whole and works hard to keep it around.

What about nuns who spend their life in prayer?

If a nun is happy praying, her gift is wonderfully welcome. If she's not happy, no gift has been given.

Didn't Jesus live for others toward the end of his life?

No, he lived for the fun he could find in what he was doing. At the end of his life, he had no need of worldly support. Unearthly support was sustaining him completely. He reached that level of contentment the same way you'll reach yours, by realizing where contentment lives and making sure you have it.

What cured Jesus of his confusion?
His misery when sidetracked.

His story sounds like Mariah's.
All stories have the same soundtrack when it comes to living in comfort. Jesus found happiness from creating his own. As soon as he knew where it was, others wanted to know how he'd found it. The same was true for Mariah.

When Jesus left Jerusalem, all of a sudden he had to support himself away from the craft of carpentry. Not that he didn't fall back on it once in a while, he did, but to journey the way he wanted to, he had to be free to move on quickly. That didn't tie in well with carpentry. After careful deliberation, he told his new acquaintances that he would be speaking at a certain place at a certain time and anyone wanting to attend could bring a donation. Plenty of people arrived. Hardly anyone donated. Jesus wasn't sure how worthy his gift was yet so others weren't sure either. At first he was embarrassed, but turning back was not an option. He had to find a way to support his trip.

He couldn't succeed until he understood the nature of success. At first he thought it was the picture of others behaving as he hoped they would. Eventually he realized it was the picture of *his* behaving as he hoped others would. To solve his dilemma, he put a price on his wisdom. Then he found all those who were doing the same. Since they were happy to be paid for their wisdom, they were happy to pay Jesus for his.

After solitude, his needs changed so his policies did, too. He still had a price to pay but it was an emotional one since that's where he knew his reward had meaning. Jesus left the world of mutual support when he entered the world of autonomy. He did so by understanding what it meant to be a valuable part of the whole right here on Earth. He kept his emotions one with God and received whatever he needed wherever he was. Eventually he knew that his body was illusion so he fed the part of himself that he knew was real.

Oneness is not a worldly thing; it's a feeling. Emotion kept him nourished. To reach the point where it could, he had to seed that love from within. Then he needed the willingness to do so on a moment-to-moment basis.

How would you differentiate our world today from the world he lived in?

The picture looks very different but, emotionally, similar growth is happening. Mariah's challenge involved the concept of commerce, and surprisingly, she had an edge over her brothers in this respect—especially James and Simon—not because of any lesser ambitions in them, but because of lesser expectations put upon her. If a woman did well outside the home, it was unusual. If she didn't, who cared? She wasn't expected to anyway.

Her brothers, on the other hand, saw success as the natural way of things—an extension of who they were as men. If they did poorly, problems abounded. She succeeded where they did not, but nothing in her youth had prepared her for such an occurrence. She didn't know how to respect her talent, make it work for her in a positive way, or handle resentment from otherwise loving friends and family.

Jesus had little interest in worldly achievement so he became a natural buffer and confidant, someone who could offer advice with no personal agenda. He'd come to terms with his gift and knew whereof it originated. To help her cope, he reminded her that happiness didn't come from the number of people impressed with her gift; it came from the number of ways she could honor it.

For a while, Mariah thought it was nice to be free of all the jealousies her other siblings suffered. Later she realized that freedom was just as personally defined as everything else. She had her own way back to it just as they had theirs.

Mariah also had her moments of wanting Jesus to change. The government was declaring war on him and he didn't seem to care. Regardless of how Mariah felt, Jesus knew what he needed and nothing she said could change his mind. She didn't think he was loving her the way she wanted him to, but his way of caring eventually taught her more about love than her choice would have. She gained a better sense of her own wisdom as she witnessed what happened to Jesus from trusting his.

From the perspective of others, it seems that Jesus' last few days were not very pleasant.

Maybe that was the point of it all—to demonstrate that happiness doesn't come from what others give to you, believe about you, or say is true. It comes from what you give to yourself, believe is true, and say is yours.

> Respect your own emotional barometer.
> Otherwise,
> You will forever be adjusting it
> To suit the whims of others.

Worksheet for Chapter 6: Mariah

How has someone taken advantage of you in the last few months?

Could you learn to say no instead, and how would you do that?

What are you afraid will happen if you do?

Who have you taken advantage of and when?

How can you get your point across without any lack of respect?

Questions to Ponder

• Who can I help to succeed with my success?

• Have I looked beyond my contribution and asked how others can expand it?

• Have I accomplished as a result of my talent or as a result of taking advantages of someone else's?

> You are the love of god.
> How are you using that power?

Personal Insights

I realized after hearing Mariah's story that I had a similar struggle. When I first began to write and the gift was still in its infancy, some people were excited for me, some not. Some encouraged me, some didn't. Some were supportive, some critical. But regardless of who was interacting with whom, one thing was clear. How I dealt with others was the dealing I got back. If I gave advice that helped a person to expand and nourish her truth, I received what nourished mine. If I gave advice that only reflected what I wanted to gain in the process, others looked for personal gain while telling me what to do. The bottom line remained: as I gave, I received. Even if intentions were misread on my part and someone was truly trying to help me, I couldn't feel that help if I hadn't been helpful to others.

7

Joses: The Humble Brother

Physical action
Takes you places without.
Spiritual action
Takes you places within.

Was Joses a spiritual person, Charlie?

Everyone here is a spiritual person whether that spirituality is acknowledged or not. You can't be here in a conscious state without spirit present. Spirit *is* your consciousness. Was Joses focused on spiritual action? More and more as he realized that physical action was ineffectual in terms of his abilities. Everyone around him was bigger.

He was Simon's twin.

Yes, and although Simon was bigger and more outgoing, both admired Jesus. Simon tried to stay close to Jesus through apery; Joses tried to stay close by maximizing their differences. In this respect, Joses had a deeper understanding of what a working union is all about.

What about James? Did he understand Jesus?

Better than he admitted, but he felt such competition that it poisoned his opinions.

When you say that Joses learned to take spiritual action, what do you mean?

I mean that he learned to trust his uniqueness here on Earth.

Will trusting myself help me to trust the people around me?

To the extent that you trust yourself—so perhaps in some categories and not others.

Why do you bring the answer back to me, Charlie?

Because to understand the world is to fathom self.

Does spiritual action relate to good intentions?

Absolutely. If you have good intentions, you attract others with good intentions. But if you want to see some action behind those intentions, you'll have to follow through. For instance, what happens if you intend to pour ink into a glass?

Nothing until I do it.

Exactly. You have to *do* in order to have.

Does the glass represent my body?

Your body is a lovely design, embracing content in matter—so the analogy works for me.

Can a glass ever change its shape?
Can you ever change yours?

In some ways.
That's your answer; but *some* is whatever each soul knows it can be. Not everyone has the same vision. As you live the possibilities that bring more meaning to your path, new ones get imagined.

What do you call this process?
God living divinity in matter.

Did Joses live his divinity?
He learned that the inside of the glass held his destiny if that's what you're asking—even if he took a while to grasp this truth. For years, he thought his body determined his destiny, and since it was ugly compared to the beauty standards of the day, he felt uncomfortable wearing it. His face was asymmetrical with eyes too small, a nose too big, ears too long, and a mouth too crooked. On top of all that, he was short in a family of tall men. Because he worried so much about his height, he tried to make up for it with girth. Comfort was illusive until he trusted that ease came from the ease he gave to others, not how comfortably others accepted him.

If we choose our looks, why didn't Joses choose a body that made him happier?
Because he chose a body that would challenge him to remember the source of happiness. At one point in his emotional history, before he came here as Joses, he used the same logic you just did, thinking he'd find more love if he had a good-looking body through which to search for it. But a preoccupation with the outer kept him from looking within. He was willing to try anything, however, and since he knew that he could, he did.

At least he chose a family where Jesus was there to help him.
And you have chosen a family with equally vital support.

If Jesus were my brother I'd be more inclined to agree.

If Jesus were your brother, you wouldn't notice anything more wonderful about him than you do about your present siblings. Jesus was helpful, but mostly by example. Joses watched him support the part of his life that was working and ignore the part that wasn't. That helped him to do the same. But regardless of what Joses learned from Jesus throughout the years, beneficial or not, Jesus had something important to learn from Joses, too—more about himself.

It began as Jesus watched Joses bemoan his shortness. In an effort to help Joses, he told him it wasn't important. But in those days, Jesus thought that change was about Joses' transformation, not his transformation. In truth, Jesus had the same problem Joses had. He didn't think he had what he needed either. As puberty approached, Jesus bemoaned the fact that none of the girls ever fell for him. Not that he didn't have love in his life. He did, but not from the girls.

What's the matter with me? he said. *Why can't I have what others have? Is God trying to punish me for something?* Mary told him that nothing was wrong with him and assured him he'd find a mate eventually. Joseph said he had years and years to pursue the art of courtship and he'd serve himself better by using his time constructively. Joses' way of handling him was to stay away. He worried though. Here was Jesus, much better looking, having trouble relating to the girls. He couldn't help but wonder what his chances were going to be.

Did Jesus continue to have this problem?

Until another focus consumed him. Everything changed dramatically when he wanted to travel. Then he began to worry about supporting a journey. When he first tried to raise the funds, he acted like no other options were open except the ones he presented—which brought him a lot of patronizing attitudes and stubborn opinions. Later, he welcomed any advice he could get. Then he faced helpful suggestions. Asked about his repayment plans, he said he would share the wisdom he'd found when he returned. To him that was enough. To others it was not. They didn't see why Jesus' priorities were more important than theirs. So even though he spoke to his parents, a cousin, and the rabbi, he had no takers.

Mary and Joseph didn't feel compelled to support any trip they didn't think was wise in the first place. But they assured him that if he needed to travel, he'd find a way to do it. The rabbi said he couldn't show partiality to Jesus when so many others had needs more serious. Levi declined rather abruptly saying that Jesus only courted him when he needed something from him. After this round of refusals, doubt plagued him even more. He knew that he had to go. Making it happen was something else.

Confused and discouraged he ruminated, trying to figure it out. Joses asked him why he didn't just leave. Jesus said he didn't have enough faith. Joses understood, plagued with doubts of his own at the time. The fact is Jesus never fully trusted his journey. He just reached the point where he couldn't resist the pull to go any longer. It was either follow his instincts, or stay miserable the rest of his days.

The best decisions often come out of frustration and the need to heal from it. Happily, his worst fears never materialized and neither did Joses'; he met a wonderful woman, married her, and had a big, boisterous family. Jesus found a way to support his journey and knew that from then on, he'd be able to travel for as long as he needed to. If for some reason his support had never come, that would have told him something important, too: that his journey wasn't as vital as he thought it was. Joses wished him well, hoping with all his heart that Jesus would find his answers, wanting so much to believe that answers could be found.

After Jesus left, Joses concentrated on the healing of others through herbs. As his depth of wisdom grew, so did his need for a place to share it. Rather than deal with this problem in an open and forthright way, he brooded and blamed the people around him, sure that they were the cause of his thwarted goals.

When he first began his practice, he had no money to pay for the cost of an office, so he took in a tenant. Although this man was honest and paid his rent on time, Joses eventually needed that space. His challenge was to figure out how to please himself and honor the renter at the same time. The option to cancel his lease came to mind, but by then the man was a friend. The guilt he would suffer from telling him to leave didn't seem worth the effort. Then he looked for alternatives. When nothing suitable developed, he felt unsupported. The problem was not the renter, however. The problem was his own lack of faith that his tenant could leave and still have a happy future. While trying so hard to meet the renter's needs, Joses thwarted his own. How do you feel when your answer is right in front of you but you don't love yourself enough to accept it?

Frustrated, angry, and confused.

Joses did too, so the renter wasn't receiving as much of his goodwill as he thought he was. To make matters worse, his patients reflected his struggle right back to him, saying that they didn't have what they needed either. No one enjoys a frustrated, angry martyr—nor does anyone want to believe that he or she is the reason for all that angst. When he finally asked his tenant to leave, the man reacted beautifully. He'd been expecting it for ages.

Did Joses feel much better having made this decision?

Yes, but living it brought the real pleasure—sort of like thinking about a shower as opposed to actually being there.

It's hard to believe that the universe supports us in whatever way we need it to.

Not if you ask why else would the universe exist?

It's such a big idea compared to me, and so imposing.

If it were smaller, would you feel differently?

I don't know. It works so perfectly—almost like a miracle.

Are you so different? Don't you work perfectly, almost like a miracle, too? The universe is your creation. It reflects everything you know to be true about yourself. Never is energy without its mirror. The universe "is" because you "are." It lives to reflect the God who created it but within that definition it actively shows you yourself.

Are some mirrors bad?

No, mirrors simply are.

What's to keep me from blaming others for the mirrors I hate?

Nothing except for the mirror of blame returning with a little extra thrown in for good measure. And the extra is there because action/reaction is such a generous giver and loves to give you more of what you asked for.

Why would I ask for blame?

Next time you're ready to give it, ask that question again.

But Jesus and Joses eventually moved on.

Yes, they moved on. Jesus knew that inside his heart, where he was happy or sad, traveling was crucial. So he left regardless of how he felt. On the first leg of the trip, he doubted his progress frequently. But if one place didn't have the answers he sought, on he'd move to see if another place did. When he still hadn't met his goals after years of searching, he found a person who challenged his focus. *Why are you looking outside for answers when you're hoping to accomplish within?* Jesus had no response. Why was he? At that point he returned to Jerusalem and decided on a different method of research. He had no guarantee of success but he knew that if one person had achieved what he was after, he could, too. Then he did whatever he thought was necessary to make enlightenment possible.

Joses got out of his stagnancy by focusing on where his needs *were* being met instead of where they weren't. As he looked past outer images and focused on inner ones, he discovered all kinds of insight that others didn't have. He had it and they didn't because of what he had lived and they had not.

Would you call his practice a conventional one?

For then it was. Conventional medicine in those days was the use of herbs and elixirs—and both were used for a multitude of ailments. Today, this is usually unconventional. But they had many types of healers just as you do. Joses' personal philosophy was that cures got handled like miracles and death got handled like destiny. He also believed in loving rapport because those who had the most faith in him seemed to heal the fastest.

Because of their mutual interest in healing, he and Jesus spent a lot of time together. Both were pleased to philosophize and attracted those who wanted to, too. Occasionally he and Jesus debated long into the night about who was right and who was wrong as both tried to prove their theories. Sometimes they agreed and shared their thoughts. Other times, they doubted that either of them had answers and wondered if they ever would.

Their relationship had its ups and downs, too, though. The downs came from a need to prove a point. Jesus came from the truth of his experience and Joses came from the truth of his. As a youngster, Joses faced a different reaction to his appearance than Jesus did to his. People were constantly saying *are you sure the two of you are brothers?* Joses felt these comments deeply and dreaded their repetition. Most of the time cruelty was not intended, but cruel in his own assessments, he felt that judgment harshly. Jesus couldn't relate. Therefore, when he told Joses what to do to get over it, Joses was not impressed. In fact, this was an unresolved emotional conflict that sometimes got in the way of their friendship.

Joses matured and a charming side of his nature emerged. As the charm worked its magic, he thought *Wow, what a revelation!* Once he discovered this part of himself, he used it over and over. Not only did it make life easier when going places with Jesus, it eased the way for Jesus on occasion.

Jesus dealt with others the way he dealt with himself—directly. His bluntness often got him in trouble. Fraternity blossomed through the merging of opposites. Each of them seemed to have what the other lacked and fusion was miraculous.

During those years of growing up, people found other ways of comparing them and Joses often came out as the favorable partner—much to his delight. Realizing how harmoniously they merged, they played their union to the hilt, performing miracles that neither of them could have done alone but together could be successful. One of them developed in the early stages of adolescence. Jesus was small as a child, too, sprouting up only when he reached puberty. Joses never sprouted. So although they didn't appear to be close in age because of their height difference, they were. In most situations people looked to Jesus as the elder. In the one that mattered the most to them as teenagers—the girls—he seemed impossibly younger.

Jesus was extremely shy and tongue-tied in the presence of female contemporaries. When he did speak up, he blurted out his feelings with such intensity, the girls retreated in awkward silence. Joses, on the other hand, never thought the girls took him seriously and so behaved like their long lost pal. He was afraid to even consider romance. Consequently, he was forever making friends where Jesus found it impossible. Alone, neither of them felt adequate to tackle this phase of growth. Together, they handled it humorously and companionably.

They also joined forces on carpentry projects. Joses had a good head for business but not for new ideas. Jesus had plenty of new ideas but couldn't fathom numbers. Therefore, whenever Jesus conceptualized a new invention, Joses conceptualized feasibility. They entertained themselves quite often this way, although Joses often abandoned his advice in the face of Jesus' enthusiasm.

Was Joses building a practice at the same time Jesus was building a following?
Jesus didn't have much of a following until he returned from solitude. His common speech patterns combined with his sophisticated ideas confused people. They expected intellect from the educated, not the likes of him. Even the few followers he did have were baffled by his rhetoric; and the bigger the crowd got, the worse his rhetoric became.

For anyone to take an interest, he had to either present his ideas more simply or speak in a way that matched his thoughts. Neither was forthcoming until he came home from the hills. Then he was able to share in a way that drew people to him. He'd stopped trying to impress others and was only trying to love them. His audience could feel the difference and responded.

His new success was another challenge for Joses. He began to doubt his healing skills in the face of Jesus'. That problem was never solved until he settled more comfortably into what came easily to him. Joses saw himself as the dull and rather conventional brother of Jesus. And since he never heard differently, he suffered from what he considered cruel comparison. If you had a sibling who was brave beyond your wildest dreams, and who took new steps every time you turned around, would you feel so comfortable being the opposite? Jesus was happy as a rebel. Joses was not, and given what Jesus accomplished being one, Joses judged himself as boring.

He had no interest in fighting the status quo. He wanted a loving family, a job he enjoyed, and friends he respected—a portrait of many people. But until he could honor those ideals, what difference did it make how many others shared them? As far as he was concerned, his parents and siblings were all over the map in their bravery—while he was very plebeian. Some folks have difficulty accepting their rebellious natures in the face of conventional families. He had the opposite challenge: accepting his very conventional nature in the face of rebellious kin. Aware of this discrepancy, he had a hard time believing that his ambitions were equally meaningful.

Many times, the enthusiasm of Jesus for his goals dampened Joses' enthusiasm for his, and before Jesus left to travel, he didn't object to that happening. Jesus was a great talker, so groups were a natural outlet for him. Joses, on the other hand, related easier one-on-one. After Jesus returned from solitude his groups were very effective. Therefore Joses felt that his one-on-one was lacking.

When he tried to copy Jesus, it didn't go well. In front of a crowd his body broke out in a sweat and his mind went blank. The other bad news was James—always there to taunt him by saying, *the mimicking twins are at it again.* Had Joses been more kind to himself, he would have remembered that Jesus hadn't always been so comfortable one-on-one. He conveniently ignored that fact while feeling sorry for himself.

As a very intense youth, Jesus found it difficult to be tactful and diplomatic. As a result, he often offended others. In a crowd, he could offer solutions without singling anyone out. But for Jesus to reach his goals, he had to be an impatient person. His challenge was to love what impatience was getting him instead of what it was taking away.

Eventually he was comfortable one-on-one and eventually Joses was comfortable with groups. The point is, everyone has a timely way of sharing. When that comfort is honored, more avenues open up through which to share. Both of their methods matched their growth. When Joses honored the man he was, the man he was got happier—and that's the best healing force that exists. The ultimate existence is one of optimism, insight, and appreciation. You must be living it to be bringing it to others. *Cause and effect* illuminates your progress on a moment-to-moment basis. The answers you need are always right in front of you, ready to be recognized and ready to lead you deeper within.

Did James pick on Joses because he was smaller?
No, but Simon did, lording it over his twin whenever possible. As a young boy, Jesus had known the pain of shortness, so he was compassionate about this—even if not about other complaints.

How did Joses feel about Jesus' relationship with their cousin, Levi?
He understood why Jesus felt so compelled to be critical, but he preferred neutrality. It wasn't his nature to take on a cause—which is why Jesus found his presence so relaxing. Joses had other concerns that seemed more relevant to his evolution.

Joses was certainly challenged.
He was. There was never a moment in his youth when he wasn't comparing himself to others for one reason or another. Nevertheless he grew up to be a happily married man, contented

father, and productive healer. Why? Because he supported his brothers in what they hoped to accomplish even in their petty jealousies. He honored their uniqueness even when his lay fallow. He valued their contributions even when he was struggling to express his own.

Joses was not what you would call an adorable child. But people eventually responded to the inner child in him that was full of warmth and acceptance. He and Jesus had many challenges dealing with each other, but they managed to merge their energies resourcefully.

Regardless of the many setbacks Joses endured in his quest to find fulfillment, the world became a haven of love as he made it a haven for others.

The best test for action/reaction is to give a little love away.
It's much easier to discover the power of physics
Through pleasure and bliss
Than it is to feel it again and again
Through agony and pain.

Worksheet for Chapter 7: Joses

List the people in your life who receive your consideration.

What is it about them that ensures your loyalty?

Who has your loyalty because of a common bond and who has it because of circumstances?

Of the ones who have it because of circumstances, who are the least deserving?

These are the people you need to tend. How can you share your heart more meaningfully with each and every one of them?

Questions to Ponder

• After I leave this Earth behind me, what kind of energy do I hope to encounter—that which is full of praise for my journey or that which is looking backward to atone?

• Are my choices leading me inward toward more love and caring or outward toward more censure and criticism?

• Do I tell people how to live or do I live as I hope others will?

Bring more mastery to your life
By seeing that mastery
In the people around you.

Personal Insights

For the past twenty years, I've lived in a community that is greatly influenced by outer beauty. Therefore, the story of Joses was a great reminder that a happy and satisfying life has nothing to do with the look of the body; it has to do with the look of the soul. I wish I always remembered this, but I know I don't. I try to look into the soul of a person rather than be influenced by who that person is, but I sometimes struggle to do so. I try to keep my truth as pure as possible, but ego still interferes. I know my soul will re-create again, but I still have fears that I won't accomplish what I'm here to do this time. I hope it doesn't matter that I sometimes fail to remember what's important; I hope it only matters that I do the best I can.

8

Salome: The Beautiful Sister

The belief that problems exist
Is the belief that solutions do not.
Give value to the status quo,
And the status quo transforms.

Did Salome have trouble valuing herself?
She had trouble believing that she was more than her looks,
which made her wonder how she'd be treated without them.

She had the same problem Joses had.
Emotionally, yes. Joses felt insecure about his appearance; Salome
felt secure, but they both feared that the outer was all they were.

That's funny.

It's ironic. They had the same fear although one was beautiful and the other ugly.

Which just goes to prove something, I guess.

It proves that life is an emotional journey. Two people in the same family chose opposite looks to find the same growth.

Couldn't they have done it another way?

Their souls believed in the way they chose. The purpose of every journey is to know the essence within. Both believed that the chosen method would work.

Is everything I have chosen for that reason, too?

Absolutely.

Perhaps you have more faith in me than I have in myself, Charlie.

Perhaps you have more faith in yourself than you think you do. The soul who looks for benefits is a heartbeat away from finding them. If the search is proving difficult, look for emotional satisfactions instead of worldly payoffs.

Are you saying that worldly payoffs are not important?

I'm saying it depends. They can be, but only as a means through which the inner you evolves. To help this essence grow is to let it have its way—even when illusion seems to discourage you from doing so.

How does this relate to Salome's growth?

She had to discover who she was like everyone else. A few years after the resurrection, it became obvious that someone had to step forward with an accurate account of Jesus' life. No one seemed to be doing so and misconceptions were spreading. Salome decided that she would try. Early efforts were quite naïve but once she found her central theme, skills accelerated.

Plenty of people had more experience when it came to local

history. But Salome knew Jesus well. In this respect she was perfect for the job. As word of the project spread, people showed up with information: some from friends who had known Jesus for years, some from acquaintances who knew him only slightly, and some from people who knew him not at all. Salome had to learn to trust her instincts over anything seen or heard.

She realized quickly that lots of people wanted to cash in on Jesus' notoriety whether they knew him well or not. How could strangers write about him? Well, the writing part was easy; the accuracy part was not. Salome had to have faith in her ability to distinguish between the glory seekers and the seekers of truth. Not easy at first, but she learned to by staying in touch with her instincts—the only process that worked.

She also had to contend with the many biases women faced. Females working outside the home in anything but charitable organizations were barely tolerated, yet here she was trying to do so. Little support was given—even from her parents. They didn't want her involved in something that could bring even more controversy to the family.

What about James? How did he feel?

He knew inaccuracies were growing regarding Jesus' life and death, and he wanted a truthful story. But he was torn regarding Salome. He had all the expected prejudices that most men of his generation had. Therefore, he tried to get Simon involved in hopes that he would take over. Simon dragged his feet. When James realized it would have to be Salome or no one, he tried to be supportive.

But regardless of James and his opinion, or how Mary and Joseph reacted, Salome knew her contribution was valuable. She was shrewd when it came to other people's integrity, and she had a lovely, if somewhat untrained, illustrative talent. Staying with the project was difficult. No one encouraged her, and the person she most wanted support from didn't give it.

Why?

Because he was her husband, and not only did he feel that men were the ones to make meaningful contributions, he found it irritating that Salome would concern herself with anything other than him—or looking pretty. Under this pressure, she got to the point of saying many times, *that's it. I can't handle this project one more day.* Then someone would come along and say *I'll handle that part of it for you* and on they'd go.

Obstacle after obstacle was overcome and a curious thing happened. Regardless of how many facts Salome wanted to share, how accurate she thought them to be, or how many people believed they were true, she was more interested in talking to those who understood Jesus' process. And she was more interested because she wanted to know it herself.

Is any of her writing in the Bible?

Some of it is, but as time passed, people preferred other stories. The version Salome put together had anecdotes about the times they lived in, the people who entered their lives, and facts about his childhood and the trials and tribulations they had endured with him and each other.

She also included her memories of his final days, his message after the resurrection, and what he said to expect in the future. Lots of information arrived through other people, but proximity to Jerusalem didn't guarantee that a person knew Jesus well, or understood his teachings for that matter. Salome had to look into the eyes of the storyteller and sense the truth of what she was hearing. Then she had a better sense of whether or not to include the material.

Salome had known Jesus all her life as a well-beloved brother. Of course, she depicted him in the only way she could—as a normal human being—living his life to the best of his ability. Those who wanted to think of him as special didn't embrace her views. They supported another one—that Jesus embodied a more exclusive divinity. Surprised when people wanted to think of him as different, she suspected they did so because it offered them an excuse as to why they couldn't achieve as he had.

I can't love as Jesus loved because he had special help; he lived in miracles and I don't; he was God and I'm not. She also wondered if they felt that way as compensation for the loss they experienced after Jesus was gone. Her goal was to honor his memory and never include material that suggested he thought of himself as the least bit different from the rest of them.

What did people think about his divinity after he returned from the dead?

To believe he was divine then was easy. He'd done the seemingly impossible. The hard part was to think of themselves as he did: as the love of God. He didn't want to be thought of as special. His life had been a testament to the opposite. He'd understood from an early age that many before him had lived their enlightenment here on Earth. In order to believe that he could, too, he had to have faith that his chances were equal to theirs. The last thing he wanted people believing was that their chances were less than his.

Salome's book was written slowly because she grew up in the process. When she thought that the love in the world would only spread if her material got shared, pressure accelerated. Nevertheless, she continued with her crusade regardless of how many well-meaning friends and family told her she'd taken on a hopelessly impossible task, and regardless of how many detours and disappointments she endured along the way. In this respect, the project showed her the nature of growth. It proved that reward didn't come from whether the book got accepted or not; it came from accepting herself as she created it.

How is a person supposed to remember that needs are fulfilled from within?

The heart decides what is timely in terms of reminding you. You only have to love what the heart dreams up. Salome feared that her own limitations would diminish the project but it turned out that her only limitations were her doubts about doing it. She only had to trust. After all, she was the one who was organizing the book. Therefore she was the one who was meant to do it.

Thank you for being so patient with my questions, Charlie.

Thank you for thinking I can heal your impatience, Betsy.

What was Salome's biggest challenge other than working on this project?

Dealing with her physical body. She didn't feel so blessed to have outer beauty when those who didn't seemed kinder, especially her sisters. They found it hard to love her in the presence of her insufferable guilt, insinuating that a person without beauty had less to be happy about. Whether it was true or not was irrelevant. She believed it was, and her beliefs created her behavior. Although her sisters had a hard time articulating their feelings, they still had to deal with her and the way she overindulged their whims in an effort to compensate them for their loss.

Salome reasoned that if they got more of everything else, she wouldn't feel so guilty for getting all the looks. She punished herself for being so attractive but she punished her sisters, too, by believing that pity was appropriate. When she got that mirror back she was devastated. Over and over people refused to see the real Salome. But they couldn't see it until she saw it. And she couldn't see it until she knew that her sisters were every bit as lucky as she was in every way that mattered.

When she married, happiness was hers for the first few years. Then she began to expect her beauty to do the fulfilling. Frightened by how that made her feel, she saw the work as her savior. But her husband didn't. He saw her preoccupation as robbing him of his leisure time with her. As he spent hours complaining about her use of time, he didn't use his own time well. Therefore, while he thought his anger was about her preoccupation, it was really about his.

Instead of confronting this problem in a forthright way, Salome told her husband that he was lucky to have a beautiful wife, and why wasn't that enough for him? He didn't take kindly to her words, even though he deserved them. Then he complained about her attitude to anyone who would listen.

His objections weren't the only ones she heard. Her in-laws were critical, too, insisting that she was shirking her wifely duties.

To her it was the proverbial in-law problem but no relationship is intrinsically negative. Each person brings a universe of action/reaction to whatever else is happening.

How did Mariah feel about Salome's project?

She was happy Salome was dedicating her time and energy to something she believed in, and she was glad that Salome had something to contemplate other than how her looks affected others.

How did the rest of the family feel?

Simon was pleased that someone else was handling the project; especially after the pressure from James. Joses worried about the accuracy of her memory—she being younger—but he admired her efforts. Joseph had less interest in what she was doing than Mary. He was bothered by the bickering of Salome and her husband. No matter what they seemed to argue about, it always came back to her use of time. Mary knew that Salome had finally found a way to be taken seriously and worried that she might become obsessed.

What else was included in Salome's project?

The message of Jesus after the crucifixion: *You are the love of God in full and adoring divinity whether you recognize that power or not. Nothing can destroy the magnificence of your soul and I am living proof of that ideal. Answers appear as soon as you open your heart enough to feel them. Nothing within one's truth is hidden to the eyes of love.*

When he returned to speak with his friends after the resurrection, Salome was blissful. She felt all the love in him as her body communed with the love of God and lost its need for matter. It was as if Jesus were saying to her, *Bring your body to the oneness from which it birthed—the food for everlasting life—all of its needs are handled.*

Many people felt the power of love that day. Later, it wasn't so easy. But Salome knew that having felt it once, she could again. When people tried to convince her that Jesus had been the source of all those feelings, Salome disagreed. She knew that emotions couldn't be conjured up simply because someone wanted her to have them. They were hers because she had kept her thoughts where love could truly blossom. Some called it brainwashing. If so, it was the most delicious cleansing Salome had ever experienced. So wonderful, in fact, that everything she did from that moment forth was to keep the feeling alive.

I don't suppose Salome asked Jesus if he would come to visit her again.

As a matter of fact she did. This was a question on the tip of many tongues that day, not just hers. He said that he would since once you know how to play this game of matter, you want to play it rather frequently. It would happen, he said, from her own need to feel his love.

Many times he spoke of the concept that everyone is a receptacle of godly light. Therefore it was only logical that he would reveal himself when she had forgotten that truth. He promised that he would return as the Jesus they all remembered in terms of his heart, if not in terms of his body.

What does that mean, Charlie, in terms of his heart if not his body?

It means that it was up to the people he left behind to recognize his heart in the person they faced. Salome was sure she would. Alas, she got fooled, and more than once. Even though he was there, she wasn't aware of it. Like many, her eyes and ears blinded her soul. Each time he came to help her, he came in a body that stirred up all her prejudices. Even though she thought of herself as liberal and unbiased, he caught her where she wasn't. This is how she learned. What is missing is never felt. What is never felt is still unknown. In that space where love is not, something else is happening. Mirrors never falter, however, so as she shunned instead of loved, her heart dropped out from under her as she felt the shunning of others.

That's coming to the problem through the back door. It forced her to go through pain without even knowing she'd turned her back on love.

Maybe so, but until she could see the beauty in every encounter, she couldn't go through the front door. Jesus made a promise to her and he kept it. He came to her; once even to help her with the book. Right up to the house he walked and knocked on the front door. When she saw him, she couldn't imagine this person having anything valuable to offer her. Not because he came in another nationality, an abhorrent body, or a different religion, but because he came as a judge.

Her hate for these men was so intense she slammed the door in his face. Nevertheless, the few words spoken were well remembered. He said he was present at the trial and had information she might want to hear. One look at him and all her prejudices came storming to the surface.

This was a miracle in the making for the more Salome questioned the meaning of that visit, the more she wanted to search for this man. She told herself she was only seeking him out because of how little she knew of the trial. The true creator was that niggling voice, suggesting that perhaps her hostile attitude had ruined the very dialogue she sought.

Salome went to the only place she knew could offer help: an office where clerks located government officials to assist in resolving issues. Ignored at first, she doggedly hung around until someone finally listened to her. He was monosyllabic and rude, sensing the presence of someone in hostile feelings—her mirror, of course. She gave him a description of this rather youngish judge and, exasperated, he told her that no such person existed. Years of experience were required to attain this position. Then Salome realized how easily she'd missed the obvious.

On the way home, she was sure she could hear Jesus saying *caught you on that one, didn't I, Sal?* Salome felt encouraged, though. Jesus was keeping his promise. He was around, he was coming to her, and he would continue to remind her of what it meant to be this God in full understanding of oneness.

Then Jesus didn't look like the Jesus she remembered.

If Jesus had looked like his old self, he would have been easy to recognize. Where was the growth for Salome in that? He was challenging her to see past the look and sense his heart—her only meaningful reality.

To whom did he give this promise of returning?
To all who wanted his help.

Will Jesus help me this way if I ask him to?
He will, and so will other beautiful souls.

How will I know if any of them are around?
If your heart is filled with judgment, you won't. If it's filled with love, you'll think that everyone you encounter is one of them. Remembrance is not about effort; it's about recognition of mirrors.

Was it fair of Jesus to come as a judge?
He never said he was one; he simply dressed for the part. She assumed the rest. His message to her was that he'd been at the trial and had information relevant to her work. Salome only had to let him speak. That didn't take effort; it took acceptance that he was a person telling the truth. He was there for her when she needed him. She had questions; he had answers.

Salome was tortured by the possibility that Jesus had found himself in a situation that he hadn't intended to live. What if he deeply regretted his decision to stay around and now couldn't help himself? Her visitor wanted to tell her that Jesus looked like a man who knew where he belonged and was happy to be there. Therefore, as Salome looked for information about the trial, she only had to remember that fact.

I love you for all this information, Charlie.
And I love you for receiving it, Betsy.

I feel so comforted to know that Salome struggled with problem solving, too.
Who amongst this beautiful congregation does not?

I guess we always think we have the hardest problems to solve.
And for the heart who is living them, that's true. Each soul is challenged according to its blocks. Wherever light is resisting love, big challenges are happening. But since you only come here to

find more love, problems are solved as soon as you do. Emotion can't be measured in linear terms. The world you see today is but an instant in the flow of eternal thought consumption. Make your reward a renewed sense of purpose. Then your enthusiasm will alter all that your mirror reflects.

What would you say was the best part of Salome's journey?

The growth she found. She finally came to understand that nothing on the outside could bring her the security she needed if the inside felt insecure. For years after the resurrection, people wanted to know about Jesus, this man who had done the seemingly impossible. They were hounding his family for information.

Salome was a handsome woman, thrown into the limelight suddenly and irrevocably, and she wanted to leave an accurate history. To do so she had to get past her misguided beliefs that her outer beauty was the asset needed. To know the true value in others she had to know the true value of self. As Salome came to know this core, she bonded with the core in others. Then as oneness manifested, they told the story of Jesus' life.

Problem solving
Is no more complicated
Than trusting yourself.
Answers are right in front of you.

Worksheet for Chapter 8: Salome

What do you consider the best feature you have?

If you wrote down a body feature, answer the question again.

If you wrote down anything to do with your intelligence, answer the question again.

If you don't have anything to write down, then what feature would you like to have?

How can you give those features to others so the gift will then be yours?

Questions to Ponder

• Do I rely on the outer me for praise, attention, and love, or do I praise, love, and attend the part of myself that is real forever—my heart?

• Am I hoping that somebody else's love will solve my problems or am I looking for someone to love so that all my problems disappear?

• Do I judge my worthiness by how I look or do I judge it by how I love?

> God is energy.
> Energy expands individually.
> How big it gets depends on how much
> It is willing to embrace the beauty in others.

Personal Insights

Salome's story touched my heart deeply, not only for the honest discussion of outward beauty and the problems that can surround it, but also for her determination and persistence to share her contribution. I've had plenty of setbacks that challenged me to stay focused, too. Persistence and determination also played a role in my life. I've seen enough *Oprah* and read enough books to know that despair comes to everyone if the struggle feels lonely and support unavailable. For me, it was wonderful to hear that Salome, all those many centuries ago, had the same experience I had—and that millions of others have had as well: the challenge to stick to what is believed in regardless of how long it takes to put it together, how many people try to deter the process, and regardless of how many obstacles have to be overcome.

9

Mumu:
The Controlling Grandmother

To bring more kindness
To others,
Is to act autonomously
To the betterment of self.

Was Mumu a nickname, Charlie?
Yes, but everyone used it. Kaarjbian was her real name, which
stood for a person of exceptional beauty, inside and out. She was
neither. Since Mumu hated being reminded of the void she lived,
she was happy to leave it behind her.

Whose mother was she?

She was Joseph's mother, and while he tried to honor the role she played in his life, Mumu made that difficult. Misunderstanding the nature of power, and believing it came with control, she tried to control anyone she could—including Joseph.

We all want to feel autonomous, don't we?

I know I do, but autonomy to Mumu meant having the last word, so she tried to have it in every conversation. The harder she tried, the more she got rejected. The more she got rejected, the more she wanted power—power over others, power within, power to control her environment, power anyway she could find it. *If others choose to be free, they'll choose to be free of me. How disastrous!* Few people liked her anyway. If her loved ones deserted her, who would she have? If Mumu had known that power given was power received, she would have changed her tactics. To her, power given was power denied. Therefore she tried to keep as many people as possible dependent on her.

If power couldn't get her love, what could?

How does a tree love itself? It began the same way you did—as a seed that sprang from its source—and all that it can be is only more of what it already is. Just as a tree broadens from reaching for light, so does your broad and sweeping love-filled soul. The tree doesn't care if it grows up, down, right, or left; it embraces growth in whatever direction has it. Do the same and you'll be thriving, too.

A tree can be stripped by outside manipulation.

True, but the tree reseeds no matter how many setbacks it has; and so do you.

Did Mumu use this analogy?

No, but she loved the use of analogies because she loved a person using them.

Did Jesus find wisdom from listening to Mumu?

He found wisdom from realizing how wise he was to listen to himself. Mumu wanted to feel close to Jesus but telling him the devil had plans for those who challenged authority couldn't make it happen. As far as she was concerned Jesus was a brash young man ignoring his elders and forever seeking impossible goals. As a youngster he was like most children, looking for guidance, but he found so little from spending time with her, he lost interest quickly.

Did people see her as cruel?

They must have. At times she was. She wanted to feel important and it seemed to her that those with power did. But as she got rejected, she didn't feel good about herself. Trying to feel better, she criticized the rejecters, causing even more separation. Mumu wanted people to listen to her. When they wouldn't, she did whatever she could to get their attention. Part of the problem stemmed from the fact that while she was growing up, she'd been taught to be unselfish, not to be happy. An unselfish attitude made her miserable. Then she took her misery out on others.

That sounds like martyrdom.

That sounds like the martyr she was.

With whom was she a martyr?

Lots of other martyrs. Quite a few were in her family, which is why Jesus was such a challenge. He believed in pleasing himself and eventually got to the point where he wouldn't concede to her demands, or anyone else's for that matter. As a result, he was moving from gain to gain to gain from honoring his instincts. And Mumu was moving from pain to pain to pain from ignoring hers.

She wanted company in her misery.

As do all martyrs. The few times Jesus did listen to her depressed him so badly, he avoided her every chance he got. Mumu loved Jesus and wanted to see him happy but she loved control more. When she had to choose between the two, she chose control. Jesus didn't know why she was so compulsive, but he knew he disliked the person it turned her into. Therefore, he neither embraced her beliefs nor succumbed to her bullying. In fact, when pushed inappropriately, he was the most stubborn person Mumu had ever encountered. She needed agreement. When he showed signs of autonomy, she came down on him hard.

Was she pretending to be wise?

It didn't feel like pretence. It felt like insecurity. *Do as me, be as me, act as me, so I can approve of self.*

Did she believe that age gave her privileges for bossing him around?

If other methods for gaining authority didn't work, she tried whatever she thought would.

Was Jesus unkind to her?

Actually, he tolerated her with remarkable patience and then went ahead and did whatever he thought was wise. He tried to respect her views, but he couldn't imagine a philosophy making her miserable making him happy. Before he left to travel, Mumu talked on and on about his selfishness until even those who agreed with her were tired of hearing her speak. Then she tired of talking.

Why?

Because misery hates being miserable alone.

Why didn't she just forget about Jesus and concentrate on her life?

Because she didn't have that much self-respect. How could Mumu give to Jesus what she hadn't yet given to herself? Had she stopped talking long enough to listen to his longings, she might have awakened her own. Mumu was so busy ordering him around with shoulds and shouldn'ts, she had no time to consider her own shoulds and shouldn'ts.

Did Mumu blame Jesus for the lack of closeness between the two of them?

Sometimes, but their lack of closeness had nothing to do with him. She created her own separation from a lack of faith in her life and, therefore, his as well. Mumu bombarded him with advice. When he wanted to study, she told him to go out and play with his friends. When he didn't want to study, she told him to "hit the books." When he wanted to pursue the girls, she told him to stay out of trouble. When he didn't want to pursue the girls, she told him to act his age. When he tried new carpentry inventions, she told him to satisfy his customers with what they already understood. When he challenged the rabbis with new and unpracticed theories, she told him to stop being a heretic. When he wanted to travel, she told him he wouldn't know how to care for himself away from home.

No matter what Jesus decided to do, Mumu told him he'd made a mistake. She was the devil's advocate in the only literal sense there is. And because she offered such devilish talk without, she was plagued by the devil within. *You've done this wrong, you've done that wrong. This was stupid, that was stupid. This won't work, that won't work.* Negativity fell heavily on any action Mumu took because, as soon as she tried to paralyze others, she felt paralyzed.

What made her so negative?

She made herself negative. Granted, her parents had struggled likewise but Joseph had lived with her and he had chosen differently.

Some people are better equipped to honor themselves.

Everyone has the same equipment: a mind that can make a decision. The reason one person has integrity and another does not has more to do with respect than heredity. Joseph learned to honor himself by asking why he should dedicate his entire life to the whims of his mother. Believe me, Mumu badgered him a lot. Whatever he was choosing, she was criticizing. Some people follow in their parents' footsteps and some don't, but whichever is chosen is not the fault of the parents.

After all, Mumu had a son who showed her how to choose more wisely, and Joseph had a son who showed them both how to choose even more so. When you hear that crippling voice, deal with it the same way Joseph and Jesus dealt with hers. They couldn't ignore Mumu. She was a part of their lives. But they took a good look at how she lived and what her opinions produced, and found the strength to re-create.

This kind of strength comes from desire, a desire to live in serenity, peace, and fulfillment. Mumu's behavior pushed them to choose differently. Happily, they turned a disadvantage into an advantage by choosing constructively for themselves. Mumu considered her motives honorable because she cared so deeply about her family and wanted them to be happy, but you can't give happiness to others. You can only give it to yourself, thereby inspiring others to find theirs.

How did she deal with the other children?

She did the same thing to them that she did to Joseph and Jesus: come up with shoulds and shouldn'ts, and the shoulds and shouldn'ts were always the opposite of what that person wanted to do. Mary was her third favorite target after Joseph and Jesus, for Mumu knew how to prey on every insecurity that a young Mary suffered. Only Mary's knowledge that Joseph was every bit as tested as she was enabled her to cope. As Mumu got older, she didn't mellow; she got worse. But everyone in the family knew how to deal with her, so disruptions were less intrusive.

Did she have a long life?

She did. She didn't live to see the crucifixion, but she lived long enough to welcome Jesus back from his travels. From the trust he had in her, she knew he must have found great wisdom from going. In Mumu's last few moments before passing over, she realized why the world had seemed so bleak; she had listened to the voice who said it was. With Jesus beside her, she heard another voice from deep within her soul, giving her faith in a better tomorrow. As sanity returned, Mumu saw the human journey more clearly—as an enchantment for the everlasting evolution of oneness.

What does that mean, Charlie?

It means that we all come here for one reason and one reason only: to find the love within ourselves. And since the lack of love separates us from the oneness of God, the goal is to feel it again.

Why could Mumu hear this beauty then but not before?

Because she knew that her time was almost up. That bleak voice couldn't control her with any more bad news about that which had no time to manifest. Negativity only festers in a mind that wants to justify its actions and since Mumu was in the middle of an involuntary act—spirit leaving the body—it had no power to reach her. To use an analogy, suppose you were going to the beach for the first time. How would you know what to expect?

From what people told me or the pictures I had seen.

So you'd be relying on the experiences of others. After you had been there, you'd have your own knowledge to fall back on. Mumu's flash of insight could be compared to having been there. Suddenly she knew that any counsel other than her momentary feeling was invalid. You could also compare it to what happens when you take a running leap over a stream. In that moment when you haven't quite reached the other side, where is your focus?

On where my foot is about to land.

If someone behind you doubted your jumping abilities, could he interfere?

Not if my foot was about to land safely.

That's how it was. Doubt couldn't touch Mumu. Her foot was about to land safely.

How does this relate to negativity festering in a mind that wants to justify its actions?

While deciding whether to take that running leap, fear has a chance to interrupt the process. When you hesitate and ask if you deserve to get to the other side, doubt gets a foothold. Thus, you would be justifying your actions. The stream is there, so it's for crossing. If you trust the timeliness of every stream, nothing can stay your progress. Mumu didn't trust her leaping abilities, nor did she trust the timeliness of every stream. Nevertheless, the universe stays in perfect alignment—which means that whether or not you think a leap is possible, the stream will still be there, waiting for you to cross it. You're free to take as long as you want to do so. In fact you can contemplate that stream for years. It will still be bubbling along, totally confident of its positioning. It never doubts its reason for being and therefore never doubts yours. The stream knows it is where it's meant to be and so believes the same about you.

It's an analogy for all of us, isn't it?

As is all creation. Everything you see with your eyes is ripe for analogy. It's all here to reflect the hearts who choose to embrace it.

What happened when Mumu doubted her crossing abilities?

She'd sit down to ruminate. Then naturally she wanted company in her hesitation. When someone leaped over anyway, she tried to retard the vacillators. *Come sit with me and ponder. You can't make it to the other side anyway, so why even try?* She became the voice of discouragement.

When Mumu passed over, did she watch Jesus from another plane?

If you're willing to accept that another plane was simply Mumu without a body. What she saw intrigued her. Jesus had plans to leave his body now and then, while still in form.

Did he join Mumu when he left form?

He joined the oneness of his heart and she was a part of it.

What does that mean?

It means that he walked through illusion and found reality— the God in every heart.

What gave him such faith in that goodness?

He gave it to himself.

There has to be more to it; so few people live this concept.

Maybe today. There was a time when everyone could move in and out of form at will. Jesus' faith came from his certainty that what had been usual once could be again.

How many times did he do it?

Quite a few, since once he knew that he could, he didn't want to stop.

Did Mumu think of Jesus as religious?

She thought of him as a highly principled man. He believed that whatever made logical sense and worked, was worthy of his attention.

Where was the logic in believing he could do what nobody else could do?

There was no logic in terms of life in Jerusalem, but Jesus was a student of history. He didn't see himself as limited to any popular isms of the day. He believed that whatever had proven possible for one was possible for him. He reminded himself that every person who lived, had lived, or would live was the same beautiful energy. To say you are the same as everyone who has ever lived is to say you can be, do, and have whatever you've heard about, read about, or learned about, not to mention what you might think up all by yourself.

Jesus read voraciously, wanting to know as much as he could about his predecessors and exposed himself to all manner of writing—anything he could get his hands on. This was one of his reasons for traveling. What was yet to be discovered that he didn't know? Everywhere he went he studied how the people lived, what they believed in and why, where they found their strengths and their truths, and whether their philosophy worked for them on a day-to-day basis. After searching many places, he determined that there wasn't a single soul on the face of this Earth who had his answers. There were only those who had their own. Therefore, he would have to live the truth he loved and see what happened.

After Mumu dropped her body, did she spend time with Jesus?

She continued to love him through his progress. Without the

voice of negativity she was able to support him in ways that he enjoyed, too. Each of Jesus' growth spurts moved him into greater layers of light until he lived a moment of total recall. Then he knew himself as the love of God, and in the everything he felt was the everything that existed.

You experience this feeling, too, when loving your life. It's a state of bliss where joy is all encompassing, thereby making it easy to encompass all there is. Then, quite naturally, more of that wonder is what you seek. The need to expand this core is the motivation that got you here in the first place. It's also the reason the Earth was created. The universe represents the whole of energy expressing its magnificent emotion in imaginative form.

Did Jesus have any out-of-body experiences when he came to know this beauty?

He did. If you love yourself with total devotion, you love yourself as God loves. Then you're able to do what God can do.

Can you describe what that involves, Charlie?

Any time growth is happening atoms are expanding. As they do, half the fun is knowing that you direct the process. For instance, on any given day, you know yourself as a person with thoughts in the here and now but also in the past and future, all three happening simultaneously with you deciding the focus. The same phenomenon exists when you are out-of-body.

The mind lives in the past, present, and future wherever it is. As you drop the body and the limitations of matter disappear, oneness with all of creation is felt. Therefore knowledge *is*. When you contemplate broader focuses, you don't lose who you are; who you are just grows.

Jesus was in-matter and out-of-matter at the same time at the end of his journey, but so are you when your heart is filled with love. It's just that he mastered this art so completely he could shift his focus depending on where his love had meaning in the moment. Growth evolves out of who you are right now—the only path the universe knows. What do you suppose a universe would spring from?

Another universe?

Of course. All universes come from the same place—space. It's God's way of playing in matter. Energy loves itself so much, it has many ongoing games at the same time.

When I'm able to jump in and out of matter, will I know them all?

You'll know them all as soon as you jump into the feeling that all of them sprang from: oneness with all of creation.

I get a kick out of coming from so many angles and ending up in the same place.

I get a kick out of bringing all of your angles into oneness.

Did Mumu help Jesus find fulfillment?

Absolutely, she gave him emotional mirrors that helped him to know himself. As he recognized that reflection, growth blossomed. As growth blossomed, he welcomed oneness instead of resisting it and jumped over a stream. Each crossing signified a victory over separation, so each leap got him closer to his source. Eventually, every separation was handled, and he and the source were one.

When Jesus went into solitude, was he honoring the autonomy of others?

He was honoring his own; thereby placing great value on self-direction. No one thought his journey wise. By then, however, people were used to the unexpected from Jesus and little resistance was given.

Did he struggle with guilt over any of his decisions?

He struggled with guilt over all of them until he realized that energy is free to be and do as it pleases. Once he understood this truth, he demonstrated someone living it. He called it the ultimate love for self—the only pathway to heaven.

Did Mumu behave differently with other members of the family?

She was fairly consistent with all of them. Mary learned to cope with her by resorting to humor. When the children were old enough to understand that interaction, they followed her lead. Mary walked a fine line, though; she believed in honoring her elders. But she also believed that Mumu's need to dominate was out of control. She feared how it might affect the young ones. Therefore, she kept a watchful eye on what was happening around her.

It sounds like Mumu was pretty cruel.

Ego behavior usually is. She didn't think of herself as cruel, though; she thought of herself as powerful. That's how ego works. It makes you think you're getting what you want, while taking away what you most desire.

Did Mumu think of herself as intelligent?

She thought of herself as verbally adept, but the words she used were unfriendly. Unfriendly or not, they got her what she wanted—attention—so she used them as often, and in as many ways as possible. When she was a child, it seemed to her that a barb here and a barb there kept her in the limelight and entertained her family, while setting her apart as someone special and therefore blessed. Her elders thought it novel that she, a child, could sting a smug adult with a few biting words.

As Mumu matured, the need to be noticed intensified. When recognition faltered, she was cruel to gain more notice. The meaner she got, the harder it was to admit to foolish behavior. The goal was not to hurt people; the goal was to feel important. But the more she verbally abused, the less she achieved her goal and people started avoiding her instead of enjoying her. It wasn't until her journey's end that the truth became more obvious. She'd forgotten that a sharper mind only cut a bigger swath when used to reap more love.

> If you want to know the depth and breadth
> Of your journey
> Ask how deeply you go within.
> You can only take a fantasy full route
> While crediting the energy
> Who thought it all up.

Worksheet for Chapter 9: Mumu

If you leave this lifetime tomorrow, who will feel cheated of your love?

Will he feel cheated because of your behavior or because of his behavior?

If not your behavior, bless his path and move on.

If you leave this lifetime tomorrow, whose love will you feel cheated of?

How can you give that love in order to have it?

Questions to Ponder

• Am I using my wits to encourage superior love or am I using my wits to feel superior?

• When I leave my body behind and only have emotional growth to value, will I be praising my choice to come here or ruing my lack of foresight?

• Do I want others telling me how to live, or do I want others praising how I've lived so far?

> Cherish the beast in you.
> Then, at least, its worst manifestation
> Is simply feeling appreciated.

Personal Insights

I have to admit that I laughed a lot while hearing Mumu's story. It was cathartic in many ways for I had a relative with some of Mumu's tendencies. This story lightened that burden considerably and gave me a much clearer picture of the true motivations behind negative thinking. I had my inner demons to cope with as a result of that relationship and the negative grip on me was hard to release. But Mumu's story reminded me to keep my sense of humor. Now I'm less inclined to concede to those negative memories because I can think of Mumu and laugh at myself.

10

Juda: The Striving Brother

All that comes tomorrow
Seeds itself today.
Whatever you nourish in April
Brings bigger blooms in May.

That gives me something to ponder, Charlie.

Juda's whole life was about pondering it. Over and over, he struggled with *size* and what it meant to him. "More, more, more" was his motto. Not seeing the worthiness of the moment, he never enjoyed the one he had. Fulfillment was always about the future and what might happen when it finally came. *If only I had this, if only I had that* was the mantle of his existence. And he wanted more

in almost every category: personal friendships, business associa-
tions, wifely affections, parent/child relationships, career—you
name it. But he only wanted more because he feared that without
it he'd never be happy.

What part of his life did he enjoy?

Unfortunately, without appreciation, it was hard for him to
enjoy any part of it. He had good friends, a nice wife, intelligent
children, and a mission he thought important. Still, it was never
enough. He pushed himself to achieve more, pushed his wife to
praise him more, and pushed his children to please him more.
Instead of welcoming his role as husband and father, he used it to
explain his failures. Then he boasted about what he could have
achieved were his family less of a burden. Blame didn't help; it
attracted blamers back.

His wife and children avoided him whenever possible, uncomfortable around his attitude. Hurt by their absence, he rationalized his predicament with all manner of excuses to explain their
behavior. Nothing helped until he realized that he had a choice:
spend all of his days complaining about his life or spend all of his
days fulfilling the life he had. Denial ended but only after he honored the gift of the moment—the people right in front of him—
exactly the gift he needed for moving him onward and inward.

Was he influenced by Mumu?

To the extent that his behavior reflected hers—and at times,
they had more in common than he liked to admit. Both had trouble appreciating the people around them. When his brothers confronted him about his attitude, he made light of it by using the
influence of Mumu to explain the way he was—a tactic that usually
got a smile from his siblings. His wife was not amused and his children were confused.

Did Jesus try to help Juda solve his problems?

When Jesus knew how to solve his own, he did, but Juda didn't
go to Jesus regarding domestic issues. He saw Jesus as incredibly

naïve about male/female relationships. Jesus was happy enough to leave those matters to others, freely admitting his lack of expertise. Later, when Jesus returned from solitude, he knew that domestic issues were solved the same way any problems were solved—by being the other person.

Did Juda care that Jesus remained single?

No, but the fact that Jesus had so little in the world and was still excited about life irritated him. He worked harder and harder to get what he thought would satisfy his appetite, and Jesus found more and more satisfaction with nothing to show for it.

Did Juda trust Jesus' help when it came to other problems?

When Jesus returned from traveling, he did; before that, occasionally. Time was the gift Juda needed—time to stand on his own two feet and do some problem solving without Jesus' constant handholding.

Perhaps if Jesus hadn't left, Juda wouldn't have found more confidence.

If Jesus hadn't left, Jesus wouldn't have found more confidence. Juda found his by turning what he considered a catastrophe into a triumph. He and Jesus were compiling a manuscript about the history of the world and those who had sought a spiritual path. When Jesus said he was leaving to travel, Juda was devastated. He believed that Jesus needed to be around for the project to get finished.

Although Jesus warned him many times that he couldn't continue without more insight, Juda didn't take him seriously. Therefore, when Jesus set the date for leaving, Juda was beside himself. Jesus expected his anger having lived his own so thoroughly. But Jesus believed that he *was* hurting Juda and felt guilty about it. Juda encouraged his guilt, sure that he couldn't continue alone. Jesus felt badly because he still believed that loving Juda had to do with being there in every way Juda needed him. In truth, loving Juda had to do with being there for himself so Juda could learn from example.

Fortunately, Jesus had enough gumption to go ahead with his plans regardless of any resistance on Juda's part or guilt on his. Although Juda did his best to stop him, the same thing happened that usually happened when Jesus made a commitment: lots of conversation with no reversals. Jesus was easy to talk to but hard for Juda to fathom. Focused on spiritual goals, he dismissed any need for worldly gains. Regardless of how many arguments Juda used to convince him of his position, Jesus never saw any advantages.

Did Juda think of Jesus as selfish for wanting to travel?

He certainly did. His plans were being threatened by Jesus' plans. While stubbornly saying that Jesus was wasting his time in a futile focus, Juda wasted his in a futile focus. Then all that rage came out in his body. In fact, the day Jesus left, Juda injured his back, reflecting a mind that said *all the support I need has suddenly left my life.* After Jesus had been gone for a couple of weeks, Juda fell down some steps and twisted his ankle, reflecting a mind that said *I can only function at half my strength since the other half has let me down.*

That's funny.

It always is when somebody else is living proof of physics in action. It's harder when you're the one. A sense of humor certainly helps though—since looking at self is so much easier when self isn't taken seriously. After the ankle improved, Juda visited Mumu and burned his finger on a hot kettle, reflecting a mind that said *burns are the only way I can punish myself for the scalding remarks I've made about my beloved friend and brother.*

Did Juda wonder why he was so accident-prone?

He attributed it to his generally foul humor. After Jesus left, he basked in all the agreement he got that Jesus was making a fool of himself by leaving. He actually said *if Jesus had more sense in his head, I'd be free of this pain.* Jesus wasn't suffering from any lack of logic, though; Juda was. Eventually he had to ask himself why Jesus should be doing what made sense to him. He wasn't doing what made sense to others. Many considered their writing a lot of wheel spinning. They said to themselves *what could these two possibly write about that hasn't already been written?*

Maybe they didn't understand Juda's need to express himself.
I'm sure they didn't—just as Juda refused to understand Jesus.

Could Juda have willed a happier mood?
He could have. Instead he wallowed in self-pity. It quieted his nerves at a time when they badly needed it. But heartache continued so he continued to search for answers. Eventually Juda decided that he was happier working on this manuscript alone than not working on it at all. It wasn't easy at first but the inner strength he gained wouldn't have been so rewarding had the grief and anger not preceded it.

Did Jesus ever help Juda with the book again?
Not in the way Juda wanted him to. And because Juda clung so stubbornly to the old way, he almost missed the new way. He wanted it face to face. Jesus wanted it soul to soul. So even though Jesus picked up where he left off, it took Juda a while to recognize the pick-up. That could only happen as he went inside to the place they shared together—their common love for the project.

Was this a hobby for Juda?
It felt like a calling. But he worked on it in his spare time so, in this sense, it was. To earn a living, he fixed up homes that needed refurbishing and woodworked in a broader sense than Jesus. Not all the brothers were good at carpentry but all of them were exposed to it early in life. Therefore, any inherent talent revealed itself quickly.

Although Juda enjoyed creating through wood, he didn't enjoy how society perceived him—as a manual laborer. He wanted to be thought of as a scholar. Not that he was treated badly, but convinced that scholars were treated better, he was dissatisfied.

Where does respect come from? Who can give it to me? And what do I need to live in order to find it? For a while he thought the outside picture embraced his answer. Therefore he was always trying to get a picture that had it.

Is anything possible if I believe in it strongly enough?
If you're talking about emotion, yes.

Levi found what he thought impossible.
Levi's challenge was to realize that nothing in the world of matter could interfere with his gift of finance. Juda's was to realize that nothing in the world of matter could prevent the birth of respect. Each of them had their timely challenge. Although it may seem to you that life is unresponsive to personal needs, it always makes sense in terms of enlightenment.

Was Juda compatible with his wife?
In the beginning, he was. As time passed, he became more involved in the work and the gathering of material. They were equally ambitious, however, just about different things. He cared about getting ahead with the manuscript and having steady work. Evelyn cared about getting ahead in society and having steady friends. He thought she was making a fool of herself—trying to be someone she wasn't, trying to get people to invite her places and trying to drag him along to boot. Lo and behold, Evelyn thought he was making a fool of himself over the writing—trying to be someone he wasn't, trying to get others to show more interest, and trying to get her to go along on his wild goose chases after historical data.

It's too much.
It is funny, isn't it.

What happened to this project?
It got finished and shared with others.

How was his offering different from Salome's?

Salome's focused on Jesus' life and all that had followed the resurrection. His focused on what had come before, but the two were joined eventually.

When Jesus and Juda worked on the manuscript together, they both decided on content. Any disagreements were handled through compromise. When Jesus returned from solitude, he never told Juda what he thought the project needed but he always helped him to feel it. Juda didn't know how it happened at the time. Now he'd call it communion through thought. He couldn't force that union; he had to open his heart enough to sense Jesus' feedback. When they held the same emotion, that was easy.

Did Juda attend Jesus' gatherings when he returned from solitude?

Many of them. They were beautifully conceived: insightfully tender, responsive beyond his wildest imaginings, and somewhat demanding. You couldn't last long around Jesus if you didn't take responsibility as the creator of your experience. That was the only way his philosophy made sense.

Surely there are those who love his teachings but don't believe in total responsibility.

I'm sure there are. That doesn't mean they can't go deeper and find more love.

Is it possible to cherish Jesus but not believe in autonomy?

It's possible to take any beliefs you want and cherish whomever you please, but to embrace Jesus' teachings and not believe in autonomy is to ask for confusion. From the day he returned from solitude to the moment he resurrected, his goal was to individually empower. Everything he lived was to show us what that meant.

Maybe it was to reveal that he was God.

Maybe it was to reveal what it means to be this God.

Did Juda think it was possible to be everything Jesus proved to be?
No, but he eventually thought it was possible to be everything he needed to be. Jesus never told Juda to be like him. He told Juda to love himself as he was.

Did Jesus know something Juda didn't?
He knew himself, Betsy. When Juda knew himself, they were one.

What did Juda think of Jesus' resurrection?
They had discussed the meaning of enlightenment many times and talked about those who had known it before them. In a way Jesus prepared him for the same by sharing what he thought it was all about—and then by living those principles. Whatever the eyes behold has long since been conceived in thought, so Jesus brought his understanding to many, knowing that he had already paved the way for them to follow. He prepared that way as any master would—be he tailor, gymnast, or philosopher—with classes explaining his methods, examples of his work, and a book that focused on the means of his expertise. Quite a few people followed Jesus by honoring their desires.

None of them did so as dramatically as Jesus.
The term, dramatic, is subject to interpretation. Quite a few have lived that transformation and quite a few have done so publicly. Each soul chooses a path that is meaningful to its growth.

Who decides how—the conscious mind or the God within?
By the time a soul is ready to live it, they have merged.

Does the soul live in oneness as a newborn?
The newborn is aware of oneness. Each soul wants to live that union on a voluntary basis and we all come here hoping to. An infant knows the complete love of God until it senses another option and believes it. Therefore the goal is to rebirth into the feeling it knew before. You rebirth into oneness by living what it

means to feel that love. It's a feeling that comes from the heart, the place where energy revives itself. This is the ultimate experience you're here to embrace.

Can I help others to live this ultimate?

All that you give to yourself, you're able to share with others.

Could I say—all that I share with others I give to myself—and have it work?

If you're talking about emotion, yes, the heart receives what it gives. A more reliable phrase would be: *all that I have within is mine to share.* Find the feeling you want. Then you have it to give away.

But to find a feeling is to offer it.

True, but until you understand that everyone is you, this can be confusing. When oneness is evoked, the only emotion you want to give to others is your own heart's desire. Jesus couldn't share eternal life, though, until he had lived it anymore than you could share the art of tailoring until you had mastered it. Energy can only bring to the whole what it comprehends. But if you appreciate who you are at this level of awareness, you'll take that love with you into your next evolving level.

But Juda eventually shared his work.

Yes, even when others ridiculed him. It was very different from other manuscripts being offered, and he was very different from other presenters. Many were shocked that he was so presumptuous as to assume that his contribution was every bit as meaningful as the ones preceding it. Quite a few were annoyed that he saw his material as every bit as inspired as that which had been in existence for centuries. And several were outraged that he had the nerve to present a scholarly work regardless of how the world perceived the look of a scholar. Often, however, the new and untried is resisted, and often for that reason alone.

What gave Juda the courage to go forward?

Watching what happened to others with courage. As Jesus lived his ultimate, Juda knew that whatever Jesus could do, he could do. Whatever one can do, all can do. Jesus told him in as many creative ways as he could that he only needed to live his own definition of beauty because, then, he'd join all others living in theirs.

Was there any jealousy between Salome and Juda since both of them were writing?

No. Juda was writing long before Salome started. In fact, he encouraged her.

What did the rest of the family think of this hobby?

Joseph worried that Juda was ruining his marriage and letting contracts get away from him that would have secured his future. Levi pretty much scoffed at any endeavor where Jesus was involved. Joses was sensitive enough to encourage Juda, but when it came to Juda's wife, Joses was less sympathetic. He saw Evelyn as a nagger, constantly trying to get Juda to better himself. Joses said a prayer of thanks every day the he wasn't married to her. Mary and Mariah were patronizing on occasion, mostly because they encouraged Juda without really having faith in his abilities. But Juda had his challenges like everyone else in the family.

Did he think of himself as a mature human being?

Not always. In fact, he walked away from a lot of problems, well aware of what he was doing. But after making his bed, as the proverbial saying goes, he lay in it as comfortably as possible, especially considering his coping skills. His family often thought he should be doing things differently and told him so. They thought Jesus should be doing things differently, too, and didn't hesitate to tell him so either. No two paths are exactly the same, just as no two personalities are, so all of them handled their challenges from their own unique perspective.

Jesus could hold his own and not let swaying hearts affect him.

Juda found that almost impossible to do. But Juda watched as Jesus got happier from honoring his instincts and he got better at honoring his. Juda saw Jesus become a stronger, more independent, self-supportive friend to himself and learned to better befriend himself. Juda watched Jesus come to know that the God he sought was the love within his own beloved soul and got more acquainted with the God in his.

Monday, Tuesday, Wednesday, Thursday
All the love of God in matter.
Friday, Saturday, Sunday, Monday
All the whole that sings in clarity.
This day, that day, year after year
God is the love you hold so dear.

Worksheet for Chapter 10: Juda

Who in your life is so important that you couldn't cope without them?

What does this person give you that seems so very valuable?

As you look over that list, write down what you might be able to give to yourself if pushed to the hilt to do so.

Of the ones you listed, pick one to focus on.

Now how can you give it to others so the gift will then be yours?

Questions to Ponder

• Is my life meant to be a testimonial to others or a test to see how much I can honor self?

• Am I making the most of what comes easily or am I always looking for hidden and obscure talents?

• Do I see my mirror in the people I face or do I always notice our differences?

> What if
> God is color blind, deaf, and mute,
> And only responds to love?

Personal Insights

Juda's story was personal for me in that I also suffered under the delusion that if I had the perfect picture—with everything in it I wanted—I'd be a happy person. I got the beautiful home, I got the great community, I got the fabulous club, I got terrific friendships, and I got the money to make it all work. I even got the whole shebang twice. You guessed it! Happiness wasn't mine. Both attempts were built on the hope of outer gratification instead of inner gratification, and both collapsed with the slightest shift in attitude of the person living it with me. Since then, I've been building from the inside out, not the outside in, and I'm a much happier person.

11

Weecum: The Childlike Brother

Nothing valuable
Goes from one person to another
Unless that transfer carries love.

Are you saying that nothing valuable goes with a gift alone?

I'm saying that value has to do with emotion. Send some of that along with your gift and it really makes an impact. For Weecum that was easy. Retarded, his brain couldn't evaluate so he had to rely on his heart. Some would call that a handicap; for Weecum, it was an asset.

Why?

Because, in a past lifetime, his intellect had gotten in the way of his emotional goals. This time, his energy wanted to try the opposite.

Had Weecum received a lot of money, his life would have changed.

In terms of awareness, I doubt it. Weecum wouldn't have known what to do with it. His wants had no monetary value. He cared for the people around him and hoped to enjoy their presence. He related to the part of others that wasn't so complicated.

Then how were these people his mirror?

Mirrors are emotional. Any behavior grabbing his focus was relevant to his behavior.

That could be bad.

That could be informative. Stay away from judgment and you'll have an easier time assessing the feedback you receive.

What happens to the soul who is retarded?

The same thing that happens to any soul, be it genius, moron, or something in between. It moves on to another adventure to look for the love it missed before.

Would Weecum sound retarded if we talked to him now?

No more than you would sound like a four year old—simply because you have lived that experience. We all move on, whether we move on to another year or another lifetime. When Weecum moved on, he didn't take the role he played into his new adventure; he took the love he found from playing it.

Did Weecum understand the path that Jesus was on?

Not really, but he believed in Jesus, and he understood how Jesus felt about him. Further reasoning was difficult. Therefore, when life moved beyond his comprehension, his parents stepped in to help him out. With their tender council he functioned with ease.

Did Weecum believe in Jesus because Jesus became all-powerful?

Weecum believed in Jesus because Jesus believed in him. All-powerful energy is energy honoring self.

Did Jesus ever act cruelly toward Weecum?

No, but he wasn't immune to being cruel on occasion. When his mirror came back—as it always does—he only had to acknowledge his cruelty to keep it from happening again. Honest evaluation is the key because the memory of what happened improves as you take responsibility for what developed because of it.

Maybe someone like Weecum had an easier time using his memory productively.

Maybe you just aren't willing to ask how easy it is. For instance, how well do you remember the day you turned eight years old? If you'd been repeating that experience every day since it happened, how fresh would it be? The moment something happens, it exists. You either keep that memory alive or you let it go. But don't expect to remember that which hasn't been kept as an active focus whether it happened forty years ago or yesterday. And when miserable memories take over, replace them with more powerful ones.

What could be more powerful than pain and heartache?

The growth you've found from living them. Without a positive outlook, a sense of loss will defeat you. And you can't focus productively while thinking that life is meaningless. The soul doesn't come here to live in pain; it comes here to live in gain. When gain is not perceived, pain is felt. No one wants to admit to choosing pain, however, so blame is chosen instead. Once you acknowledge the gain, you won't want to relinquish responsibility; you'll want to applaud your efforts. Assume your rightful identity: the powerful God Almighty—eternal creative being—expanding in the chosen game of the moment.

What brought Weecum the love of God?

His memory.

I need a better answer. One that gives me hope for a better future.

A good memory is what hope is all about. Without your worthy memories, you'll be stuck in the opposite; who did what to whom, and why—a futile focus where passive aggressive behavior stains the present, taints the future, and keeps your growth at a standstill. Believe me, Weecum had his share of torturous memories. Life was hard in Jerusalem. An unresponsive government not only kept the poor humble through fear and subjugation, it kept them liable for everything thought to be wrong in the world. When laws got broken and scapegoats needed, the poor became suspect, children got beaten, relatives jailed, and friends killed.

Weecum couldn't comprehend such cruelty. The social and political climate was way beyond his ken. His parents tried to protect him but that was impossible. They lived with prejudice all around them. The people they knew were the targets of it. He had to rid himself of bad memories by replacing them with happier ones. You must do the same. If, instead, you build on what you think went wrong, vengeance becomes your focus. Vengeance doesn't end pain, it creates pain.

Are you against people working on their problems, Charlie?

I'm against people making the problem the center of their attention. Focus on the solution. You're here to heal the soul. Any direction deeming you helpless or victimized is not going to work; it's going to keep you in darkness where negativity rules. *They did this wrong and they did that wrong* warps your memory so badly, you forget what was right about your unions. And since the only reason you chose to be together was to love and release, you miss that growth when you don't.

When Weecum focused on things that disturbed him—and plenty of things did—he was upset all the time. When he focused on things that made him happy, two parents with lots of tender compassion and brothers and sisters who cherished him every day, peace displaced any anger. Others may have seen him as foolish in his affections but they were mistaken. He just knew that love felt better than any other emotion.

If you moved on to a new job and spent all your time grieving over a few sad moments in the one before, could you have any fun? It's important to remember that atoms split regardless of what they're splitting into.

Then what's the good of going back to my youth as a means of therapy?
The good comes from finding all the good reasons for living it. Hasn't it gotten you to this moment of greater awareness? And isn't that worthy of praise?

Well, yes, when you put it that way.
How else can you put it if you want a happy tomorrow? You don't have to understand why destructive patterns are with you in order to heal them. You just have to remember that blame, frustration, and anger keep that healing away. Focus differently and new patterns emerge.

Plenty of times, Weecum wished for things to be different, but that only kept him believing that someday, when he was more this or more that he might be happy. He couldn't ignore the drama but he could direct his thoughts away from the pain and toward the love.

It's easy to talk about Weecum healing; he isn't here trying to do it.
Whether he is or not is irrelevant. Healing is an inner process regardless of where the soul happens to be. The voice of futility that keeps you from trying must be handled. It is the voice that was honored when the soul first capitulated. It happened when something other than love was thought to be real. This negative force has had many names throughout the ages: ego, Satan, Hell, Hades, doubt, fear, and many more. The name you give it matters little. Recognizing it and dealing with it matters greatly.

It blows my mind that Weecum could be disturbed by this voice, too.
Don't make energy special and different and you'll deal with ego as others have before you. To know the origin of ego, you only have to ask when and why it originates in you.

Wasn't there a moment in history when it first began to rule?

Only for the soul who chose to acknowledge it. Ego will tell you anything to get your attention, even promise miracles. *You are less than the almighty God so listen to me if you want some power* is what it says. But would you listen to ego if it offered you any less? You must decide the nature of miracles and then you must decide which voice has them. Ego deals with events in matter and how impossible they are to maneuver through. Love deals with emotion. And love says *forget about matter and go for the feeling. Everything births in the heart before it births into matter.*

How does the mind fit into this equation?

The heart and mind are one when the will decides to love.

What am I looking for in terms of enlightenment?

The thought of self-endearment, whatever brings it to you.

Is it ego that pushes me to move on to new places, people, and activities?

That depends on why you're moving on. Love moves you on because you're drawn to something. Ego moves you on because you're resisting something.

I wish the concept of ego were more specific.

It is specific, just not the same specificity for everyone. A miracle for you could be an ego trap for another. Would you be so happy doing what a few of your friends find enlightening? Retarded or not, Weecum's struggle was not so different from yours. Ego said, *look at this, look at that, what about this, what about that, she did this, he did that, don't do this, don't do that.* While he focused on all that ego had to say about the picture of life, he missed what his heart had to say about love. *Where is your gift?* ego said. *Look at everyone else and what they have. What's the matter with you?*

He came here in a loving soul with no earthly ambitions. He simply wanted to embrace the people he found and enjoy the life he chose. Yes, we all have a gift, but why isn't the thrill of aliveness enough? Would you rather be with a genius who made you miserable or a simpleton who made you happy? The sweetness of his soul was irresistible, and since people expected nothing more, the gift was warmly received.

Weecum was slow-witted but very little escaped him. He just distilled that information differently. His strength was that of trust. Therefore, when the rest of the family argued over the cruelty of this or the cruelty of that, he thought about the love in this and the love in that. He followed his instincts; the only knowingness he had. The circumstances of life were way too complex for him to decipher but emotions were easy to feel. He understood the difference between happiness and sadness, comfort and pain, and kindness and cruelty; and he was free to elect or reject either one. In fact, with limited intelligence, he had a mind less capable of torture than many others around him. He only had to respond to the tug on his heart.

Weecum's family often wished for the same faith in others that he had—and they often wondered how he maintained it. But he only dealt with emotion and always tended to love. As it all came back, he had no reason not to have faith. I'm not saying that Weecum wasn't challenged. I'm also not saying that his family wasn't challenged when it came to coping with him. But by the time he came along, they were better at handling life's little surprises. Not that his parents weren't ambitious for their children; they were. But it was obvious from the start that he hadn't come to compete at the same level of intellect. He was a questioning child but his curiosity focused on the feelings of others, not on the pictures they were living. In this respect, he and Jesus shared a mirror that kept them closely connected.

How did the people outside his family treat him?
     As a special kind of specimen.

How did that make him feel?
     It made him feel uncomfortable. Therefore he adopted a viewpoint that he must indeed be different. If so, he should appreciate

that difference instead of hating it. Surprisingly, that wasn't so difficult. The words he heard puzzled him anyway so he reached out to the compassion he felt. Although his body lacked the same intelligence his mind was missing and functioned under the same limited faculties, he could talk well enough to converse. In fact, he had some very nice talks with Jesus. Weecum loved to be told all the good reasons for being Weecum. And it seemed that no matter how many times he asked for more reasons, Jesus always came up with new ones. The truth is it doesn't matter what the soul chooses to live—only that it find good reasons for doing so.

How did Weecum perceive Jesus?

The same as he perceived all his brothers and sisters—as a doting sibling.

Was Jesus kinder or more compassionate to him than any of the others?

Weecum saw caring devotion in the eyes of all those around him.

Why were they all so serene with him?

Because he made no demands on them. Weecum was content to receive a tender smile and a soft caress. Don't you think it's easy to cherish those who love you unconditionally?

Yes, but it's rare.

Not when you hold this mien for yourself, it isn't.

That was easy for Weecum. He couldn't figure anything else out.

True, and for a soul who wanted to experience unconditional love day in and day out, didn't he make a wonderful choice?

But there's so much more to experience.

What if there isn't? Can you think of anything more wonderful than unconditional love for and from everyone?

That's worth considering.
The next time you're having trouble in a relationship, consider it again.

Didn't his siblings ever come to Weecum in bad moods?
Sure, but it was his unconditional love they were after, not his opinion of their problems.

Did anyone ever get mad at Weecum?
If they were angry at their own ineptness, yes. If Weecum had been judging ineptness, he felt their anger deeply. If he hadn't, it blew right past him.

Did he miss Jesus after he left to travel?
So much so that he cried every time he thought of him. He sensed that Jesus had left his life in a way that wouldn't repeat itself. Although that proved to be so, their reunion was all that he could have hoped for. He just couldn't fathom that merger until it happened. To him the moment was everything.

Isn't that what we're all trying to do—live in the moment?
This lifetime sure helped him to do it.

Was Weecum able to meaningfully connect with Jesus?
That depends on what you call meaningful. Could he philosophize with him? No, but they shared a warm and loving affection that pleased them both.

Was Weecum around when Jesus was crucified?
His presence had left form by then.

Maybe he missed something important.
Maybe energy knows where it needs to be.

But it brought such love to others.
To the person who could figure it out, I'd agree. Weecum's timing was flawless, I assure you.

Did Weecum remember Jesus when he came home from his travels?

You bet. He had an inordinately good memory for loving attachments.

Did this come from being slow-witted?

No, it came from being slow to forget the hearts he cherished.

This certainly was an unusual family.

Was it so different from yours, or have you forgotten how individually love can be expressed? This is a journey through release. Find how your family has challenged you to give it. There will never be a moment when energy doesn't seek further implosion within. You are here to know yourself. To know oneself is to know who lives within and what that energy feels. As you release yourself from the strain of judgment—and all that judgment begets—you feel the part of yourself that wants to love. As you recognize and honor that beauty, it explodes. But it doesn't explode outwardly, it explodes inwardly—or implodes.

Why wasn't Weecum's story recorded earlier?

It was, but the same thing happened to his story that happens to any story that's ignored. It is forgotten until that recollection is meaningful. A memory is forgotten because the mind is filled with other memories. As soon as you understand why your past has not been appreciated, you'll know why it happens to the mass consciousness as well.

What am I supposed to do with all my garbage history?

The first thing you can do is to give it a name with reverence instead of mockery. Call it the love of God in search of self.

But I'm only trying to release unpleasantness.

Release doesn't kid you into a different experience. You have to turn your history into something you want to remember. Then life is seen through a lens of gratitude and there is nothing to get rid of.

Why does it have to be that way?

It doesn't. It can be any way you want it to be. But don't expect to live in the auras of those who do appreciate their histories if you don't. Look for personal gain; then you'll see humanity's.

I can look back and see how I grew from a certain person or situation, but it takes distancing to see the wisdom of a trauma an hour ago.

If you're willing to remember that everyone is you, it won't be difficult at all. It's as simple as saying *I am that person. Can I be honest and recognize self?* As the mirror is seen and understood, the gain is found.

What if my trauma comes from an earthquake, fire, or hurricane?

The mirror is not about outside events; it's about emotional investment. After it's over, ask how you felt when it happened.

Did Weecum have another name?

He had a long string of names. Most people used this one.

Is his name in the Bible?

Not today. But the present-day version is not the one that first got embraced. Is there anything in the current one about Jesus' family?

Very little.

Would you be pleased if the Bible had more information about his family?

It would probably humanize Jesus.

Then perhaps it was deleted by those who didn't want him humanized. New information is emerging because you always face your mirror. What do these stories give you?

Faith in the presence of God within all.

And isn't this belief gaining momentum here on Earth?

What are Weecum's hopes and ambitions right now?

To help as many people as possible remember why they are here—especially since it took him so long to remember. Before his life as Weecum, he lived in hundreds of other experiences in hundreds of different bodies. Among his many choices, he was a sea captain, slave, and king, and his soul fervently hoped to remember the love of God in each of the dreams he took.

As a sea captain, he thought he'd feel it in the freedom of that journey. As a slave, he thought he'd feel it in the humility of that class. As a king, he thought he'd feel it in the mightiness of that position. In every role in between, he thought he'd feel it in the emotional content of that particular focus. Not until his role as Weecum did the cycle complete itself. And since a completed cycle is one in which the mind embraces the divine will of the soul, this was the journey that worked. Few considered him wise. Kind, yes. Pure, yes. Generous, yes. Certainly not wise. Jesus did though. He understood the source of wisdom in all of us—love for oneself and respect for one's choices.

Did Weecum ever question his reason for living?

No, but not because he didn't have that much intelligence. He didn't have that much masochism. Where do you suppose a question like this comes from?

Wondering what life is all about.

As soon as life is appreciated, the wonder is understood. Philosophical questions are helpful or not depending on how you feel while pondering them. The soul in appreciation looks for all the good reasons it exists. The soul in doubt looks for the opposite, and if that isn't masochistic, I don't know what is. Many lifetimes were his before he felt this truth. Eventually this one took shape and all that Weecum learned from the previous ones paid off.

He lived through hundreds of different dreams before he knew that love could be found in any vision he fancied. Answers came from testing. Then when destiny arrived, nothing else appealed. From choosing this one experience as Weecum, everything else he'd lived made sense. So even though his mental growth couldn't comprehend the ultimate as Weecum, his emotional growth knew it all. Then, as he started to leave the human game, the only memory he had was full of love for mankind. And in this one thought he saw his reflection forever.

Trust your broad and sweeping emotion
As the only prize of worth.
Then your broad and sweeping emotion
Will satisfy your birth.

Worksheet for Chapter 11: Weecum

Write down what you wouldn't have in your life were you not the soul you are today.

If nothing in that list has the word "feeling" in it, start over.

What feelings do you value?

Welcome to the world of reality. List all the ways you can bring that world to others.

Use your imagination to dream up more.

Questions to Ponder

• Am I honoring what I can do and who I can be or am I focused on what I can't do and who I can't be?

• Am I appreciating the people with me or am I pining away for those who aren't?

• Am I praising the courage I've managed to find in all that I've lived so far or am I finding fault and keeping failures alive?

Only a grateful heart
Knows why gratitude is preferable.

Personal Insights

After hearing Weecum's story, I thought a lot about my story; how quickly I get caught up in believing that outer achievement is the measure by which to judge my journey; how easily I forget that emotional growth is the ultimate evaluation as the journey comes to an end; how easy it is to forget that what I perceive as a handicap has been leading me to the true purpose for which I came here to live; how easy it is to forget that I don't take anything with me when I leave the body behind except for the love I found while in it. And how easy it is to forget that although the picture I experienced was often hard to endure, the inspiration that followed truly changed my life.

12

Joanna: The Pretentious Sister

Nothing gets you into more of a quandary
Than pretending you have what you don't.
Not only does it thwart your needs in the moment
But it puts you into a future
Where needs are never met.

In the phrase above, are you referring to material things we have or don't have?

Sometimes. Pretense is pretense regardless of where it's directed. It's just as pretentious to say that you own a house if you don't, as it is to say that you own a concept you don't. Joanna tended to see the world through her own idealized version. If others balked at her vision, she worked harder to impose it. On principle, her goal was to keep the family aligned more comfortably, while functioning within the parameters of *acceptable*. In reality, she demonstrated a person living the opposite—someone disgruntled with the people around her and aligned with the unacceptable. Until she could be more honest regarding her own persona, she lived in pretence.

How did she align with the unacceptable?
By not accepting her family as they were.

If she didn't have what she needed, how was she supposed to feel good about it?
By loving what she did have.

Ignorance feels awful.
Which is why she resorted to pretense in the first place. To get out of pretense, she simply needed to believe that her relatives were the vision they needed to be, and the vision they were was fine.

Did Joanna make it obvious that the ignorance of others bothered her?
When she wouldn't deal with her own ignorance, she did.

Why are the two related?
Because her soul didn't waste time in focuses that weren't. She was bothered by ignorance because she refused to face her own.

What was she ignorant about?
Every member of the family, with the exception of Weecum. She made it impossible to know them well as she focused on who they weren't.

How would you describe Joanna's personality?
As self-righteous. She was always launching prolonged argu-

ments with her mother over domestic issues, with her father over discipline issues, and with Jesus over community issues. She liked to involve herself with the people around her and when she met opposition, she did her best to counter. Joanna saw herself as a good person and qualified to judge the bad. When haughty attitudes returned, she was surprised. *I'm not leading people astray, for Heaven's sake. I'm merely asking them to live a godly life.* Justified or not, pompous criticizers were in her presence again and again. She couldn't for the life of her understand why.

Being a mediator in and out of the household kept her at loggerheads with Jesus fairly regularly since he was emerging as a convincing mediator himself. He wasn't any more aware of why they bickered than she was. Only later did they both realize that they dealt so badly with each other because they hated in the other what they hated in themselves. And rather than look within to explain that discomfort, they looked without to explain it. Eventually Jesus focused on what the two of them had in common instead of what they didn't. Joanna continued to nag.

When he came back from solitude in a state of utter contentment the likes of which Joanna had never experienced, she asked him how he'd found such bliss. He said he'd discovered the seat of power, and once that seat was established, creating from it was easy.

What is the seat of power?

It is the God within each feeling heart. The mirror helps you to recognize how much of that beauty you welcome.

Is it mandatory that mirrors get diagnosed?

No, mirrors are simply tools to assist you in your search for oneness. If you stay aware of them, they teach you about your feelings. If you don't stay aware of them, they come back anyway. After Joanna received enough unpleasant reflections, she began to stay aware.

Should everyone use this theory to understand life?

Everyone should use whatever theory works.

Joanna sounds like Mumu.

They both wanted to control the people around them, and they both believed that unless they did, they wouldn't get what they needed: Mumu—a place in the family; Joanna—a place in society.

Is that why she cared so much about Jesus and his activities?

Yes, Joanna convinced herself that his behavior determined her quality of life. She wanted to be seen as respectable and she thought his activities prevented that from happening. In her opinion he was causing a lot of stress for her and the rest of the family. Naturally, she wanted him to acknowledge that fact and do something about it. In his opinion he only created stress for himself and likewise for everyone else. When Joanna rebutted, blaming him for all the criticism coming their way, he said that if he was the creator of their experience, then they were the creator of his. She couldn't have it both ways—always playing the victim. Either all of them were creators or all of them were victims.

Joanna got around his logic with some of her own. When she blamed others, it was because these people needed to shape up and behave like the normal people she approved of instead of the slaves, dictators, and rebels they were. When others blamed her, it was because they were ignorant of her goal. She certainly didn't see herself as a perpetrator of pain. She saw herself as qualified to judge the good and the bad, and qualified to make that distinction. Jesus didn't think it was up to Joanna to judge anyone; only to behave as she hoped others would.

Quite honestly there were moments when Joanna toyed with his logic. But he wasn't living it all the time so she didn't take him seriously. When he returned from traveling, he was more credible. He *was* living his theories. From his example, she was more willing to consider that, okay, perhaps the world did live in reflection. But remembering this in the middle of chaos was difficult. To help her stay focused, Jesus said to picture everyone as an energy-arc going out into the universe in all directions attracting light beams of similar activity. Sure enough, his image did help for it reinforced the concept that incompatible properties don't mix, like oil and water, fire and ice, and rudeness and respect. Joanna wasn't always aware of her hurtful attitude, but she was aware of her suffering. That was the only signal she needed to reenact immediately.

As a young woman, she was a bristly sort with a chip on her shoulder. Her chip told people to shape up if they wanted her friendship. Because she saw herself as good, righteous, and pure, she saw those who behaved differently as the opposite. Seeing herself as altruistic, she justified her behavior and didn't consider the consequences. The universe, however, doesn't discriminate between those who feel justified in what they do and those who don't. She got what she dished out whether she thought she deserved it or not.

The voice who got her in trouble was the one who said: *some gifts are important and some aren't, some jobs are valuable and some not, some of this matters and some of that doesn't.* Since she saw herself as having the *good* job, the *good* gift, and the *good* focus, she told herself that others should learn from her. In fact, when it came to family, she caught herself saying over and over *I'm only doing this because I love you. I'm only telling you this because I care. I'm only being honest in order to help you.* Beware the person who paraphrases honesty. It doesn't need to be explained. Honesty is felt quite easily without a single word spoken.

What did a person have to do to prove herself to Joanna?

He or she had to demonstrate how a union would benefit Joanna—not an attitude conducive to friendship. Friendships developed when Joanna changed her reason for having them and stopped focusing on how people could contribute to her life, and started focusing on what she could bring to theirs.

Was Joanna upset by the many disagreements she had with Jesus?

Yes, but the pain went deeper than surface irritation. She

hated to hear people say, *who does he think he is, always stirring up the populace? Why don't his siblings shake some sense into him? When is he going to do something respectable instead of push people to demand their rights?* Jesus wanted to understand the nature of power and how to rule his inner world. He wanted to know why he was here, what he could contribute, and how he was going to do that—a quest many young people share. But he was trying to bring about change by getting others to do things differently instead of doing things differently himself—the same dilemma Joanna faced.

Like her, he was pushing others to do for him what he refused to do for himself—live independently, think independently, and act independently. Instead he was living at home with his parents while telling others to be self-sufficient. He was acting like a rebel while telling others to find peaceable change. He was asking others to agree with his principles while telling them to think for themselves. When he finally realized that his present stance wasn't working, he looked for one that would. It came as he grasped the reason he himself followed others—because they were living happily in their beliefs. Therefore, he decided that he would have to get happy in his to make any impact.

Was Joanna still struggling with control when Jesus returned from his travels?

She still had expectations of perfection. When she shared that need with Jesus, he said that he was looking for perfection, too, but he finally realized that it couldn't be found in the things of this world; everything here was temporary. And it couldn't be found in the people he knew; they were all unique.

Did Jesus forgive Joanna for the scrapes they'd had in the past?

He didn't think there was anything to forgive. He knew he'd only faced his mirror in her. He found this theory of emotional give/receive by observing human nature, not only in those around him, but himself as well. Before leaving home, he'd attracted the same kind of rebellious, overturn-the-world kind of fanaticism he preached. Upon his return, he attracted the same gentle conversation he initiated. It was quite a revelation for the people around him.

Were his old friends still out there rabble-rousing?

Some of them were and they certainly had mirrors of kind. Later, when Jesus returned from seclusion, he wasn't debating anything. He was enjoying his friendships with a reverence never before demonstrated.

What is that about?

Living as he hoped others would. When Joanna asked him if he'd found his answer to perfection, he said he had. And much to his surprise, it proved to be the simple appreciation of his own energy.

Who had the hardest time with Jesus when he came home from traveling?

James. He saw Jesus as a rival again, a person capable of wooing away his followers. Simon also had a hard time because he didn't know what to make of the obvious transformation in Jesus, or how to evaluate his role with the new role Jesus had taken.

What about Levi?

He was relieved that Jesus no longer bothered him.

Did Juda have a reaction?

He tried to persuade Jesus to join him again in the project and showed him what he had done in his absence. Jesus was thrilled for Juda but explained that he now had other priorities.

Did Jesus live with his parents after seclusion?

Briefly. Then he found a room to rent. Shortly after that, two friends presented him with a house as a way of saying thank you for what they perceived as the healing of their child. Jesus said he'd simply reminded that soul from whence it had originated.

What did he do with this house?

He used it to love others. Many people lived there off and on. Even Joanna went to visit. She'd lapsed back into her "hell-bent on getting others to change" mode and hoped that a visit with him would heal her of that setback.

Did his guests ever confront each other?

Sure, but as soon as the feuding parties remembered to look at themselves for the reason they had a problem, they found a solution.

How could Jesus be sure that his visitors would always be willing to look within to find the help they needed?

He only had to make sure that his willingness to do so continued.

Did things ever go wrong?

If you mean, did the mirror ever break down, no it didn't.

Did he ever get uneasy about his visitors?

By then, Jesus knew that he only faced himself when it came to emotion. Therefore, he only had to stay at ease within. When Joanna came to visit, she learned that true caring was the respect she gave to others, not the respect she demanded back. Respect can't be demanded, forced, or extracted. It is, was, and always will be an emotion felt when given.

Didn't some of Jesus' friends betray him?

Some of them forgot the nature of illusion and tried to find safety in that which couldn't render it. But Jesus didn't have any mirrors from that kind of behavior. Mirrors are emotional. Those in betrayal played with others in betrayal. Jesus faced the love that he gave.

It's hard to believe that Jesus could be so philosophical facing a painful death.

Why—because if it happened to you, you would suffer? Many times Joanna saw Jesus cringe at what she was living, and many times she wondered how he could stand the life he'd chosen. Nevertheless they each believed in their choices.

How did Jesus find this belief?
Tell me what you know how to do very well.

Knit.
If others told you that you didn't know what you were doing, would you believe them?

No, I know exactly what I'm doing.
Their statements would fall on deaf ears, then, wouldn't they? Your faith in this ability is unshakable. Jesus' faith in his abilities was unshakable, too. He understood how to take his body in and out of matter. He mastered this feat the same way you mastered yours—with lots of time and patience. He figured out what he needed to do in order to accomplish his goal, what it would take to do so, and then he put his determination behind that manifestation.

My mastery is something I learned with my hands. His was something that changed his life.
Mastery is mastery. Your hands know how to knit because your mind understands the process. The mind teaches the body in every category.

Did Joanna understand what he had achieved?
She understood that he had a very broad definition of divinity, and she saw it as very appealing. She didn't realize he could come and go in and out of form until he resurrected, but that doesn't mean he hadn't shared his process. He had—with anyone who was interested. He told Joanna several times that he had mastered the game of matter and he was only here as a figment of her imagination. She didn't know what he was talking about. But he assured her that when she was ready to know he'd show her. And he said her readiness would come as she understood her own imagination.

How would Joanna have reacted had he disappeared in front of her?

How would you react if someone performed this task for you?

I guess it would depend on how I felt about that person.

Otherwise, you might feel fear? Perhaps the kindest gift you can give to a soul is the wisdom it's ready to grasp in the moment. Before Jesus left to travel, he had done many things that frightened Joanna. After he returned from solitude, his understanding of love and how to use it was the very reason she trusted him so completely.

How could he defy the laws of the universe and do what he did?

When Jesus learned how to cross back and forth, he was living the laws of the universe, not defying them. Perfect unison with the whole is how this universe operates. Look around you. *Matter* comes and goes on a fairly regular basis, doesn't it?

Only when it births, dies, or is destroyed. Not when it just feels like it.

How do you know? Do you understand the feelings of a tree? The world of matter exists through the soul's need to experiment. Form is not a permanent state. It disappears as the conscious mind reunites with the whole. Since the whole is where all knowledge resides, you know everything the whole knows while in it.

Jesus had a strong pull to know the whole of himself. Once he acted to back up that desire and felt the effects of doing so, nothing less would satisfy. Then he joined all others living the same enlightenment and together they celebrated oneness. But oneness is found from joining what it means. Relate it to your comprehension of knitting. How would you describe that artistry?

It's a process I understand. Therefore whenever I want to use it, I have it and I can.

Isn't this the path that a pianist knows with his instrument, an athlete with her sport, or anyone with a gift that is nurtured through pleasurable discipline? Getting to know oneself is no different. Information about oneness comes from within. Therefore, this is where the focus needs to be. If you want to know this wonderful love, find a quiet moment, gather your material together, keep your body comfortable so aches and pains can't distract you, and start to create. After Joanna heard how Jesus did this, she decided to try. She got to know herself better, too. She didn't come and go in and out of form in the body of Joanna, but since then she's done it many times in whatever form she needed.

Did she come back as other creatures or other people?

She came back as other manifestations of love. If the mission required a human form, a human form was chosen. If the mission required a creature's form, a creature's form was chosen. Whichever it was, she took the memory of wholeness with her. Therefore, she could return to it voluntarily.

Why didn't she come back as Joanna the way Jesus came back in his body?

Because there was no reason to.

What kind of reason did she need?

One that would love and cherish her expansion. The concept of oneness was fully grasped when Joanna truly understood that mirrors always reflected—not only when they felt comfortable, but also when they didn't. After Jesus left and she was alone in her effort to become enlightened, she knew that any help would have to come from within—the same way Jesus found his help.

The first sign of relief came as she stopped complaining. Happily, as she closed her mouth when the urge to condemn began, at least she didn't have the carping of others to contend with. Breaking old habits was difficult, but after she stopped fussing over the obvious waterloos of others and put some inquisitiveness into her own bogged-down, knee-deep-in-mud-position, his theories began to work for her. From then on, she looked to herself to solve her problems and learned that help came from deep within her own acknowledged conscience. As Joanna became accountable, she was able to take her first steps into honest evaluation and make friends with the mirrors she hated. Getting to this level of awareness was neither quick nor easy, but once momentum began, ease accelerated.

At first Joanna dreaded the possibility that growth depended on revealing her frailties, but after she brought them out into the open and took an honest look, she was a soul who owned those weaknesses instead of a soul who was run by those weaknesses. Then she realized that she had nothing to fear except forgetfulness.

During this takeover process, Joanna asked herself what she hoped to accomplish. *I want to be loved by my family, valued by my friends, honored by my elders, and admired by the administrators with whom I work.* What she actually lived prevented that from happening. She considered a few here and a few there as worthy of her attention. To heal she had to look at the snubs she received and find the snubs she'd given, admit the slighting she received and find the people she'd slighted, evaluate the back-stabbing she received and find the people she'd back-stabbed. You could compare it to that immediate rush of relief you get when you know why your car isn't working. Knowledge is so powerful, because once you know what is wrong, you know how to fix it.

Did Joanna use this new awakening?

Yes, it proved invaluable in her handling of all the children who arrived at her husband's institute for the handicapped. Her gift to them was the healing force that inspired new efforts. Weecum influenced Joanna greatly because she could see more clearly into the heart of an innocent because of him.

As time passed, she still watched the people around her slip and trip but her attitude was different. When she moved out of dread and fear, and into compassionate understanding, she had the same consideration to spread around.

Which of her siblings did Joanna feel closest to?

Her confidant was Joses. He had a wonderful quality, which allowed Joanna to open her heart without feeling judged. She also felt close to Weecum but discussions of any depth with him were impossible. She could identify with Juda because she understood his need to be respected. But Juda's wife, Evelyn, was her closest female friend within the family—both having similar goals. She wanted to feel closer to her mother. And Mary, like Joanna, wanted her family accepted within the community, but she found Joanna's bossiness hard to endure. And Joanna, feeling her mother's disapproval, found Mary hard to endure.

Did Joanna's journey feel wise to her?

Not always, but she learned so much from this journey that she wondered why she'd ever doubted the process. Most of her anguish stemmed from the fact that she felt alienated from the very people she thought she was supposed to love—her family. They clashed again and again over how they defined their rights and wrongs. It seemed to her that the only idea they agreed upon was that tastes were individual. And they only agreed upon that because otherwise life in a family that size would have been intolerable.

Joanna couldn't find wisdom from constantly focusing on what she considered outrageous—and most of the time that was Jesus. He cared naught for her opinions, or anyone else's, for that matter, and carried on in his own inimitable style. While trying to deal with his over-zealous approach to reform, she turned to Joses for comfort. If he didn't make her feel better, she'd sit with Weecum for a while. Even in his limited capacities, he seemed to know the difference between unconditional love and loving with expectations. Weecum saw his siblings as varied in their needs, but welcomed all of them with an open heart and a trusting soul. With his example of absolute acceptance, Joanna grew to find more in herself.

Honesty is creation
In touch with itself—
Not your opinion of what others are doing.

Worksheet for Chapter 12: Joanna

Write down ten ideas that you are absolutely one-hundred-percent sure are true.

Cross off the ones related to the world of matter and try again.

If any negative absolutes came up, rewrite them until they feel more positive.

Write down the methods you use for getting out of the negative and into the positive.

If the space above is empty, list all the methods you agree to use in the future.

Questions to Ponder

• Do I offer support because I hope to see a change for the better in others or because I hope to see a change for the better in me?

• Can the world ever find peace if I can't find it within?

• Am I looking for what I have in common with the people around me or am I looking for how we differ?

Make friends with yourself
To be a better friend to others.

Personal Insights

When I first became involved in the New Age Movement and accepted many of the concepts that seemed to be thriving there, I had an attitude pretty much like Joanna's, thinking that I had all *the* answers and no one else did. Boy, what an unattractive mirror that was when it came back and bonked me on the head!! Since then, my attitude has changed—just as Joanna's did after enough bonks. Now I know it doesn't matter what I believe in; only that I use my beliefs in a loving way. It doesn't matter if I agree with other people's philosophies; only that I honor the right to have the one you want. It doesn't matter if the world seems destined for war; only that I live the peace I hope the world will have.

13

Abraham:
The Embarrassed Brother

What you live this lifetime
Won't be remembered
In terms of names, places, or events.
It will intuit through
A heart who loved,
A soul who blossomed,
And
A visionary who believed.

Names, places, and events must have some meaning to offer.

They offer whatever they teach you in the moment they exist. After that, they're either a memory or nothing. To know what really happened, history must be considered in the context of growth—since it only existed for the wisdom it brought to those who lived it.

If growth is your criterion for truth, which names, places, and events can I trust, Charlie?

Perhaps conflicting data is the incentive you need for trusting yourself. This is how Abraham eventually found his help.

I want to be able to say, "Yes, that must be true because so-and-so said it, too."

With this criterion for truth, you will be forever changing it. What guarantee do you have that so-and-so won't change hers? Comforting though it may be to think that different souls are receiving the same tender messages, tender messages can't be heard; they are felt. Each soul interprets truth according to how it views reality. When Jesus spoke of the history he remembered, it was not the history Abraham learned in school. Embarrassed by that discrepancy, Abraham made fun of Jesus in hopes of minimizing their connection. He hoped that his friends wouldn't hold it against him that Jesus was his brother.

How do I know if the feelings you attribute to Abraham are correct, Charlie?

Correct for whom?

For those who receive it.

All who receive it have their own feelings from which to create.

Then how can they believe what is shared?

They only need to believe how they feel.

If everything comes from within your ability to remember the stories as they were told to you, how can I be sure of their accuracy?

Don't try to be. Enjoy what you have found from trusting your own heart. If others mistrust these messages, they can find ones that please them more.

Maybe they won't want to challenge what is written.

Why not? I'm challenging what a lot of others have written. The only difference between a soul who lives in bliss and a soul who doesn't is the honor it brings to self-revelation. Abraham had the same fear of controversy. Rather than take a position and stand behind it, he let himself be cowed. As the youngest child, he suffered a lot of teasing at the hands of his siblings. To them it was playful roustabout. To him, it was painful bullying. Angry, he took to his room and wouldn't come out for hours at a time. As he matured, he minded less. But regardless of how old he got, he was still the youngest in this particular hierarchy—and he had many challenges because of it.

The biggest one came at ten years old when his parents sent him to a better school. Less financially burdened and more established in the community, Joseph could afford an education for him that he couldn't give to the others. In this environment, Abraham found a way to excel, not as a brilliant student but as a brilliant strategist. With a focus on accent, appearance, and accuracy, he found a niche for himself that no one else in the family had. What began as a way to impress his siblings became an urge he couldn't control.

The more he focused on self-improvement and rising above his class, the less he resembled his family. Rather than try to bridge that gap, he basked in it, thinking he'd finally found a way to intimidate them. Not that Abraham didn't endure some serious anxieties, especially when it came to his fellow students. He walked a tightrope between who he really was and who he wanted to be. When he felt disapproval from any one faction, he rebutted with more of an attitude to hide his insecurity.

What would have helped Abraham to see more goodness instead of creating more separation?

A willingness to see it even when others did not. In fact, that's when seeing it counted the most. Whatever he saw in others he saw in himself.

I don't suppose anyone creates bad karma on purpose, Charlie.

Bad karma is simply the heart forgetting to love. Since the word *bad* is bound to keep you from looking within and finding growth, call it *the evolution of mirrors*. Karma is only the truth you're living now. As soon as you love the moment instead of resisting it, the moment transforms.

Does everyone have a gift to share when coming here?

Everyone has a heart that can love and everyone is free to use it. Abraham focused on what his eyes could see instead of what his heart could feel. He didn't realize that a smile from a passerby was every bit as valuable as a book, recital, or painting. Wanting to feel *important enough to matter,* he judged those he deemed as less. But *important enough to matter* means having a heart that's big enough to care.

To be a good person, did Abraham have to like his antagonists?

No, but after he saw himself in them, he liked himself better. People don't need to be liked by you to be released by you. Release enables you to like yourself and love for yourself is where your gift resides. The word *good* has no universal definition. What you consider good and what I consider good could be totally different concepts. Love is revealed through honesty since honesty is read by all, and anything read by all is welcomed by all. That which is welcomed by all is the love of God.

Won't I like myself less by identifying with those I hate?

You like yourself less in deception. And deception occurs when mirrors get ignored. Once you're honest about deception, love returns to cherish you.

Did Abraham hate anyone?

He hated quite a few. Between the government executioners and the populace in need of revenge, there was no shortage of candidates.

Could the murderers of Jesus join oneness as fast as Abraham if they sat in the truth of their mirrors?

Since God only lives in the moment, yes.

What does that mean?

It means that God doesn't judge choices. God sees each moment as necessary in the evolutionary process. Therefore, as soon as Abraham was honest about the moment, regardless of what it was, he lived in the oneness of God.

What about past sins?

Past sins are only that which you have deemed as wrong. Even though the mass consciousness has a definition today of what that represents, the mass consciousness of the future may disagree. Time has a way of redefining sin and what it means.

Does time relate to mirrors?

No, time is illusionary. Mirrors exist in reality. And reality is the love that is felt within.

If mirrors are always accurate, Jesus must have crucified someone.

Jesus did crucify someone. He crucified ego. Everywhere he went he slew ego right and left, here and there, in every heart he faced. Why wouldn't ego have come back to slay him?

What does that mean, "he slew ego . . . in every heart he faced"?

It means that ego is slain by the force of love, the only thing powerful enough to do it. Ego has no defense against love since love speaks to the heart and ego speaks to the picture: *Don't love him because he's too short, too tall, too fat, too thin, too rich, too poor, etc.* Ego can't compete with the force of love because ego can't think up anything that love can't automatically handle.

Later in life when Jesus had tested the power of love and knew how it worked for him, he wanted to share his truth—that God is the love within all of us. When he lived his truth, ego could flail around, get revenge, hate individuality, scheme and plot against oneness, and still come up empty handed. Ego had no power when Jesus knew whereof he originated. This is what Jesus said to his accusers: *Do anything you want to my body. Love is a thought, not a thing, and I will see you shortly to prove it.* Ego did what it could to kill him in thought. When that didn't work, it took the only route it had left. But once Jesus left form, he simply regrouped to fulfill his word and demonstrate that matter follows thought, not the other way around.

The love in Jesus grew so big and powerful that ego had to look for an equally powerful way to counter. This is how it works in every moment of history, personally or internationally, in your life or another's. Ego kills the love. This negative force hounded Abraham in terms of Jesus. *But are his predictions accurate, but has he spoken correctly, but are his theories believable?* Abraham forgot that fulfillment wasn't about Jesus' reliability, credibility, or believability; it was about his.

Are you saying that everything in this book may or may not be so?

I'm saying that it doesn't matter. If you put the book aside and couldn't remember any of it, would you lose the feeling you got from reading it? Ego will go to any length to kill the love in your life, and believe me, it told Abraham exactly what it's been telling you: *Where did Jesus get his history? How do I know if it's true? What if his version doesn't coincide with other versions? How can I trust his use of the language?*

While focused on all these worldly details, the joy in the message was overlooked. Growth is real. Everything else is illusion. If someone comes along and challenges every detail in the book, will it still be valuable to you? And how can you possibly satisfy your needs while comparing them to the needs of others?

When Jesus returned from the hills and began to preach in earnest, ego had a field day. It pushed Abraham to question Jesus' credibility by pinpointing every little defect in his speech. Jesus was self-taught, presenting his ideas simply in everyday phrasing. To Abraham, spirituality translated into complicated theories that only the most sophisticated could decipher. Therefore, ego was forever telling him that Jesus couldn't possibly have answers to ultimate wisdom. Ego kept telling him that right up until Jesus came back from the dead.

Abraham wasn't so intellectually inclined, but he thought that those who knew a lot were or should be. He only conquered his doubts through a slow realization of what the resurrection referred to—the life within not the life without. He didn't live the same rebirth Jesus did, but he came to understand the trick that ego had played on him to prevent one; making him think that renewal referred to outside gains not inside gains.

I don't have a soul resurrecting to help me with ego lies.

You have your mirror. If lies are coming toward you, lies are going out from you.

What would that look like?

What does honesty look like?

It doesn't have a look. It has a feeling.

Perhaps this is your answer. If you aren't comfortable, ego is around.

Was Abraham close to any of his siblings?

He could identify best with Juda's wife, Evelyn. She cared about improving their place in society. When she tore into Juda at family gatherings, admonishing his behavior and trying to refine his ways, Abraham supported her, even if only by nodding his head in agreement. Joanna shared Abraham's slant on life as well. Abraham admired Levi for his accomplishments in business, even if he didn't like his roughness. But Abraham was a moody child and a moody young man, which made him unapproachable.

This family was certainly a big one.

It wasn't considered big in those days. Most families had as many children as they could conceive. Disease and pestilence cut the numbers down quickly, so propagation flourished.

Did disease and pestilence come into this family?
Abraham's life ended this way.

Was he very young?
While he lay dying, he thought so, but what he perceived as the end of the journey merely turned into another new beginning.

Did Abraham believe in the resurrection?
He believed it possible, having known his own brother to live one, but he doubted that he could create as powerfully as Jesus had. And for a while, he wasn't even sure he wanted to. *So what if Jesus resurrected?* he said. *Look at what he had to go through first.*
Abraham's relationship with Jesus was not a strong one. When he was young Jesus was away. When Jesus returned, Abraham didn't know how to measure the man. Barely into his teens, he wanted the outside to illuminate greatness since that's where he thought his own revealed itself.

What did people think of Jesus?
There were as many opinions as there were witnesses to his life.

What constitutes a witness?
Anyone there.

How do you explain your witness?
The same way.

Is this your version of what happened or the version given to you?
It's a combined version. Without my input or the input I was given, it wouldn't be coming to you.

Is it mandatory that a soul be alive in a body to know a moment of history?
It's mandatory that souls be alive, but no moment exists that you haven't been alive, in-body or out. Joining the memory of

historical moments is as simple as joining the whole in which they reside. Like everything else, interpretations vary, since God is too uniquely inspired to settle for less.

If Jesus wasn't around in Abraham's youth, when was his presence felt?

From the beginning. The whole family talked about him and his letters were a constant source of information. When Abraham was young he thought of Jesus as quite heroic. He'd faced down the powers that be in his household and did what he wanted regardless.

When Jesus returned, he was a stranger to Abraham and Abraham was wary. He did watch him, though; first, out of curiosity and later, out of disdain. They grew up in the same family but their experiences were very different. To Jesus it didn't matter. To Abraham it did. In Jerusalem, those with an education were given higher status and considered wiser for having it. Jesus lived a philosophy that nothing worldly could gain you entrance into the kingdom of heaven. Therefore, you needed to look beyond it for Eden to manifest.

Abraham couldn't understand why Jesus was chosen to relay such messages. From outer appearance alone, others were better suited. Eventually he realized that Jesus had chosen himself, and the only qualification needed was desire.

Maybe Abraham expected too much from Jesus by wanting him to look more wise and learned.

That wasn't expecting too much from Jesus; it was expecting too little of himself. To believe that a look could reveal more wisdom was to hope for the same in himself. That kept him asking if he looked like a wise and learned person. This was expecting too little because there's so little wisdom to be gained from that expectation.

Was Abraham patronizing toward Jesus?

On occasion, but instead of reacting to it, Jesus reminded him that his image held a secret that would reveal itself as soon as he forgot to care about it. Jesus compared Abraham to the butterfly. *While in the cocoon,* he said, *that beauty can't be seen but it is still around to be felt.* Abraham's appraisal of Jesus wasn't quite so generous. He used to say he was only kidding as he'd make some caustic remark about Jesus' less than fashionable taste, less than fashionable manners, and less than fashionable words. Then someone would come along and blast Abraham about his less than this and less than that. In fact, it was the very courage Abraham saw in Jesus that compelled him to bring Jesus down. He listened to the voice who said: *the only way to be braver than Jesus is to make him less than you in some way.* So naturally he picked on what he considered his obvious flaws.

Jesus knew of Abraham's struggle and helped him by demonstrating that it's possible to live one's instincts whether anyone likes them or not. But Jesus didn't bait him by refusing to change; he cherished him by remaining steadfastly loyal to his own intrinsic nature.

Abraham wanted to feel important, but trying to make Jesus feel less important certainly wasn't the answer. Every deficiency he saw in Jesus, he saw in himself. His loss of faith was gradual, not an overnight fall from grace, but the impact was just as devastating. As a child Abraham lived as a cherished member of the family. As he grew older, it didn't take long to notice the many inequities in life and, much to his chagrin, plenty of them were in his. For one thing, most of his classmates had parents and relatives with fine educations, while in his family he was the first to receive one. For another, most of his friends had lovely homes to go back to, while his was modest, plain, and crowded. And lastly, most of his friends could buy whatever they wanted, whenever they wanted, while he was on a strict and limited allowance.

Jesus and his visibility challenged Abraham as nothing else could have. As he apologized for Jesus' perceived inadequacies, he felt less adequate. As he made fun of Jesus' word usage, he worried about his own. As he doubted that Jesus could possibly know as much as the learned scholars before him, he lost faith in his own scholarly achievements.

Not until Abraham worked as a tutor, assisting other children in need of schooling, was he able to use his talent productively. His mission was to help as many students as possible receive an education that, otherwise, they wouldn't have had. Then they got their heart's desire and he got his—a lot more self-respect.

Did Abraham do this after the crucifixion?

Not immediately. He had a hard time after the crucifixion. Positive that Jesus was headed for destruction rather than reconstruction, he wasn't prepared for what happened. Suddenly every value he had seemed meaningless. With little maturity to fall back on, and a deep sense of loss, a mental breakdown followed. Abraham struggled with the part of himself who wanted to love Jesus and the part who wanted to put him down. You have the same sweet challenge in your life: to respect and honor those with different issues.

Did most people love Jesus?

Many people loved him. Some hated him and some were indifferent. People hated him for the same reason they hate today: they feel threatened. And instead of looking within to explain that fear, they look without. When you think the "without" is causing you pain, the next logical step is to get rid of it.

Most of those in a panic were those who worked for the government, or saw themselves as friends of government—with much to lose if justice found new meaning. Events were not progressing as the Roman senators wanted them to. Because these men looked to the lives of others to explain their problems, they looked to easy targets like Jesus.

As scrutiny increased, ambiguity in Abraham grew. He wanted to support Jesus because he knew he was innocent of all the charges against him. He also wanted to reject Jesus; tired of the many embarrassments his notoriety was bringing him. Jesus challenged many people this way—some who knew him well and some who didn't—in large part because he refused to live the expected. As far as Jesus was concerned, he was merely demonstrating his version of love. Held up against the crucifixion, Abraham thought his version weak and ineffectual, mostly because Jesus' version has to be lived to be believed.

When Abraham tried to trust that Jesus knew what he was doing, ego screamed in his ear: *he's a fool headed for irreversible destruction, and if you aren't careful, you'll end up in the same web of suspicion.* Abraham didn't even know what Jesus stood for philosophically but that didn't stop him from fearing guilt by association. Many of Jesus' friends and relatives were watched and spied upon toward the end of his life, not to make any great discoveries, but to make a statement: *the government will not tolerate rebellion.* While fretting over this drama in illusion, the wisdom in reality eluded him.

What does that mean—the wisdom in reality eluded him?
It means that the wisdom of these events, and what they meant to Abraham was missed. Ego said *look at how foolishly Jesus is behaving.* Love said *forget about his behavior and look at yours.* Ego only cared what *others* were doing. Love only cared what he was doing.

After the resurrection, when Abraham couldn't cope with the outside picture of life, he had no choice but to look within for answers. To gain perspective, he went to Jesus' friends. Since they'd endured a lot of their own confusion, they were happy to help him with his.

He had to deal with guilt, though; seeing himself as partly responsible for Jesus' death. He hadn't stood by him. In fact, when he heard the rumor that Jesus had promised to return three days later—should he die—he told people Jesus was crazy. When Jesus returned, he was the one who felt crazed. The breakdown happened shortly thereafter.

Mood swings disturbed Abraham; highs discouraging introspection and lows discouraging praise. He was always asking what he could wring from his experience instead of what he could bring to his experience. The constant striving in illusion, or the picture of who he was, left him no time to investigate his heart, or the soul of who he was. Into this very illusionary mind-set, he met the influence of Jesus, a man who believed that a heart in action, not a body in action, revealed a person's truth.

The difference between their outlooks wouldn't have bothered Abraham so much had his been equally satisfying. But every time he turned around, Jesus was finding more contentment from living his philosophy and Abraham was finding less from living his.

Jesus knew something he didn't—that the material world had no capacity to reward. Reward came from appreciating the matter at hand. Abraham finally got through his depression by focusing on what Jesus had told his friends to do: *Find the benefits from what you have lived instead of reliving the frustrations over and over.*

> As soon as you think
> That someone else has to change
> To make you happier,
> The answer to happiness
> Is lost.

Worksheet for Chapter 13: Abraham

Write down the most important goals you have in life.

Cross off any that involve other people, or, that involve the consent of other people. Then list some more.

If your goals have more than five words describing them, try again.

If you're still having trouble, write down a few happy words.

These are your goals. These were your goals before you came here and these will be your goals when you leave. List as many of them as you can.

Questions to Ponder

• Is it important whether a person lived as a goat herder, king, or fool if his legacy brings more love into mine?

• Am I honoring the people I call important or am I hoping to hear how important I am?

• Does my future depend on what I see with my eyes or what I do with my heart?

A sweet caress and thoughtful gesture
Is the only history of record.

Personal Insights

I'll hazard a guess that most people have suffered embarrassment at one time or another at the hands of a relative. I'm certainly no exception. And you know what—I've probably caused embarrassment to plenty of mine. I'm not saying that any of us were justified in our feelings anymore than Abraham was, but to me, justification is a *so what*. Emotionally we both suffered and realistically, we both had to deal with unpleasantness. Happily, I gained more tolerance from living through those ordeals and, hopefully, my relatives have too. As the future unfolds, I try to remind myself as often as possible that I'm not responsible for the behavior of others any more than they are responsible for mine.

14

Isaac: The Blaming Cousin

Life works for you
The same as it works for your car.
It runs smoothly and
Goes wherever you want it to
When every component is honored
As an equal contributor to the whole.

Did Isaac forget that concept?
He forgot that contributions were meaningless if all they ever
offered was blame.

How was Isaac related to Jesus?

He was Levi's brother; not like him at all, however. Isaac had no interest in business or anything else that Levi seemed to thrive on. Unfortunately, he didn't know what he *was* interested in. The rest of the family was impatient with him, sure that if he wasn't careful, he'd end up with nothing to show for his presence here. To them, the worst scenario was occurring. Isaac was stumbling from one endeavor to another without discovering any abilities.

Were he and Jesus friendly?

They were cordial on most occasions. Isaac suffered the James syndrome. He also feared how unfavorably he compared to his brother, Levi. *At least*, he said, *Jesus is struggling with purpose, too.*

How did he support himself?

He took menial jobs to keep himself alive. In the meantime, he attached himself to whomever he thought an appropriate mentor. Eventually, Jesus took that role, and when the connection was made, Jesus was more tolerant than most. He knew that Isaac didn't understand the principle of working together as a whole. So although he often felt irritated with Isaac as Levi did, he tried to help him by not allowing his neediness to dominate their relationship.

Are you referring to the principle of equal contributions making each whole work?

Yes, but a principle alone can't make anything work. Acting on it can.

Some participants are not that worthy, Charlie.

Maybe not to you, Betsy, but they wouldn't exist if they weren't needed, and need is equivalent to worth in the heart of God. Just as the different parts of a car contribute meaningfully to the whole presentation—and just as the car loses power when one part is ignored—so does your vehicle lose power when any part of your whole is ignored.

Does this theory work when it comes to thought, too?
All thought deserves equal reverence if that's what you're asking.

Even horrible thoughts?
Horrible is only a judgment you demand.

Some thoughts are not that inviting.
Then give them a better welcome so they will be. If that doesn't work, see how horrible you can get them before you fall down in a heap of hysterical laughter. That's what worked for Isaac. And if it worked for him, it can work for you.

Did Isaac define horrible differently than you do?
Yes, to him it was any thought with violent connotations.

Then he was right to call them horrible. God-thought is loving-thought.
God-thought is every thought that exists.

Violence is full of hate.
Once acknowledged, it's full of honesty, and honesty is full of love.

Can you give me an analogy?
I can give you one that illuminates the importance of acceptance and release. If you fill a balloon with too much air, it becomes an unfriendly toy and bursts before you've had any fun with it. A balloon needs a balanced amount of air to keep it whole and within your reach. Your body is no different; a healthy balance is needed here, too. Without balance, arrested anger hovers below the surface waiting to burst at the slightest provocation. Dealing with content is a very loving process. It's important to keep your vehicle strong and healthy, ready to support you in any way it can. Just as the balloon holds content, so does your body. If the balloon gets over inflated, it has to release in order to stick around. You have to release in order to stay healthy, too.

Then I could be shouting all manner of horrible, treacherous, mean-spirited thoughts, and God would only notice release?

God would notice the difference between a tight, cramped aura and a loose, free spirit. If you're in the former, you attract the Gods in the same emanation and likewise for the latter. But horrible, treacherous, and mean-spirited are only dangerous thoughts when directed toward others. Get the awful out through solitary release and make room for something else—the wonderful. Awful and wonderful can't co-exist. They have different properties. I'm well aware that suppression only happens when coping is difficult, but coping is only difficult when love is left behind.

Was Isaac's friendship with Jesus a comfortable one?

Off and on. Isaac had a habit of blaming Jesus when things went wrong. Then he wanted Jesus to change so things would go right. Jesus was constantly coming up with new approaches to reform, and he finally proposed one that frightened Isaac so much, he threatened to withdraw his support. But threatening to abandon Jesus was a shaky as well as aggressive position to take, for then Isaac felt the threat of being abandoned.

What new approach did Jesus suggest?

That he and a group of friends confront the senator responsible for condemning another friend to death. Isaac told Jesus, *you won't stay in my good graces if you attempt this crazy scheme.* Jesus laughed. He said he was more concerned with staying in his own good graces.

How did Isaac perceive Jesus?

Physically, as tall and slender and of average looks; emotionally, as a mentor. Jesus committed his life to reform and Isaac committed support. This was one of Isaac's more meaningful efforts to clarify his purpose. Mostly because this time, he chose closer to his heart in the name of reform. But as Jesus matured and became more aggressive in his tactics, Isaac became more critical. He didn't think Jesus thought his decisions through; and he hated the lack of communication as to why Jesus made them. Until Isaac grasped the whys of those decisions, he wanted Jesus to change them.

If Isaac didn't like Jesus' behavior, maybe he was wise to challenge him.

Wisdom doesn't come from challenging others; it comes from challenging self. Isaac wanted a scapegoat, someone to blame for everything wrong in his life. Jesus was oblivious most of the time anyway; far too busy trying to figure out his own action/reaction to bother with Isaac's.

Jesus wasn't the only one with whom Isaac clashed. His pattern was repetitive. He'd warm up to someone or a cause he believed in, only to cool off quickly when things didn't go his way. Instead of looking within to explain his withdrawal, he looked without. *He did this and I didn't like it. She said that and turned me off. They think differently and don't deserve my respect.*

At one point he actually thought that a person had to agree with him on every single issue or they couldn't be friends. More to the point, he couldn't befriend himself. Loath to look at his own fickle-hearted insecurity, he attacked it in others. Many times he said to himself *if Jesus would only do this, I could find some comfort. If Jesus would only say that, I could give more support. If Jesus would only be the person I want him to be, I could be the person I want to be.* But this kind of thinking was not productive; it put him in the company of the most debilitating energy that exists.

Why did Isaac feel so compelled to debate with Jesus? Why didn't he do what he thought was wiser?

A good question and one that Isaac might have pondered. Why didn't he just do what he kept telling Jesus to do? And why would Jesus want to listen to him if he weren't? Jesus learned this wisdom long before Isaac did and stopped talking about that which he hadn't committed to himself.

Jesus made the same observations about his behavior that he made about everyone else's. Therefore he knew why he faced confronting natures. Isaac didn't, and instead of doing what Jesus did to understand his mirrors, he blamed anyone he could find for the ones he hated. This is how he failed himself—by listening to the voice who said: *He's the one, she's the one, they're the ones. Look everywhere but at yourself.*

How did Levi feel about Isaac's support of Jesus?

At first he was angry; later relieved. Levi knew that Isaac lacked a sense of purpose, but he also knew that Isaac could be a leech in his desperation to find it. Trying to help Isaac was exhausting because no matter what Levi came up with, Isaac always excused his failure with blame—either a boss, a co-worker, or the job itself was at fault. Therefore, when Isaac aligned himself with Jesus, Levi may have been irritated but he was also amused. *Good luck to Jesus,* he thought, *he'll need it.*

Were Isaac and Levi ever good friends?

No, they weren't compatible. Isaac wore his poverty like a martyr; Levi wore his success like a warrior. Isaac kept a focus on reform; Levi kept a focus on business. Isaac was spiritually inclined; Levi was practically inclined. Isaac prayed for a better life; Levi worked for a better life.

After many promising starts going nowhere, Isaac decided that Jesus had a platform worthy of his support. When he told Levi his plans, Levi wasn't surprised; one more fiasco like all the others he thought. He doubted any significant changes would happen regardless of what Isaac did. In fact, he thought that hanging around Jesus would only encourage shiftlessness.

Did Isaac and Levi argue?

Only in that Levi told him how silly he was to expect reform without political backing.

Was he right?

From his point of view, yes, but Isaac saw the world through different values. Ego was the voice that got between them—saying that one couldn't be right without the other one being wrong.

How can I recognize ego's message?

It's always trying to puncture holes in the balloon with jab after jab, threatening health and wholeness. Ego tells you that healing comes through separation instead of how it truly does—through unification.

I hate ego, Charlie.

Then it's winning its battle with you. Ego doesn't care what makes you hateful, only that you are. You can ignore it. But even if you don't, nothing terrible happens. In fact, ego gets you closer to love by showing you where love is not. When you think about it, how could energy ever know the full gamut of emotion unless it tried everything? Yes, ego wants to destroy the good and the beautiful, but even if it does, that win is only temporary. As far as the soul is concerned, any path that teaches you the unlimited nature of thought is worthy. Understand the moment. Then you have the option of making it better.

What if I judge the moment?

You'll be with others who judge theirs. Judgment stays with you until you're willing to release it. While it waits to be released, it goes underground in what you call your subconscious.

If it's underground, it's out of my life.

How can judgment be out of your life if it's just below the surface waiting to express? You can't deal with something you haven't acknowledged as present. You have to take the balloon into your hands, untie the opening, and let the air out. If you fill the balloon with more and more air and never release, pressure builds until the balloon has more air in it than it can comfortably hold. And everyone knows what happens to an over-inflated balloon.

What's the difference between ego jabbing holes in the balloon and me letting the air out?

It's the difference between autonomous action and being acted upon. One is done to help you feel better. The other is done to create more fear. One is done to create a timely release. The other is done to you unexpectedly. One is done to keep you in balance. The other is done to keep you off-balance.

A person only suppresses when coping is difficult but coping is equivalent to acceptance. Healing comes as soon as you ask why a certain emotion is horrible in the first place. Yes, I know it's probably because someone told you it was. But who is that someone else? Isn't it just another soul searching for love? Why would that somebody else be more of an authority on okay feelings than you are?

Some religions teach that they know better.
What is a religion? Isn't it just a body of people—people like you?

Yes, but what if they've reached a higher level of divinity?
When you've reached a higher level of divinity, you leave the human game to expand your vision elsewhere. Energy can't keep still. As soon as it understands and masters one game, on it goes to master another. Compatible souls play together in every game that is chosen. Whether two or trillions are doing so, oneness prevails. You only have to remember that no one knows what you need better than you do. If anyone says differently, that soul is in desperate need of divinity.

What about all the concepts in this book?
What about them?

Who are they for, Charlie?
Anyone who wants them.

Do you know if they're perfect for me?
I only know if they're perfect for me. Yes, they have a viewpoint, but that doesn't mean it has to be yours.

If everyone here is sharing the same awareness level, there must be subdivisions within it.
Some are better at letting in light than others, but all have the free will to do it. Some look within to find it; some look without.

But just because a soul belongs to this or that organization doesn't mean its light is any brighter. Awareness has to do with how well you know yourself, not how well you tell others what you know.

For a while, Isaac was sure that how much he knew depended on how much Jesus knew. Then of course he thought he couldn't find what Jesus was finding if he wasn't doing what Jesus was doing. Jesus changed directions frequently. That put Isaac in limbo. Do I do what Jesus is doing now or what he *was* doing? It was nightmarish because Jesus did whatever he knew was helpful, while Isaac did the same without knowing why. Angry and bewildered, Isaac blamed Jesus for the fact that he couldn't find contentment. Jesus was doing whatever he pleased and having fun. Isaac was doing whatever Jesus did and feeling lost.

During this time, Jesus thought that the more he could get others to follow him, the more he could justify his path. Aside from that, Jesus knew why he made his choices and therefore made them convincingly. Isaac had no reason for making his other than Jesus had made them first. He seemed so sure of himself and that attracted Isaac. Jesus' beliefs weren't always so appealing, but he, as a person living them, was.

Is that why certain leaders emerge regardless of their beliefs—because their enthusiasm is so contagious?
It almost has to be the reason since enthusiasm is the link that holds us all together. As Isaac waited for Jesus to make each move, he felt more like a robot than a participant. He preferred to think that some miraculous revelation would stun him into awareness. In truth, he only needed to love the person he was and follow his heart.

The voice who did him in was the one who said *you can't achieve anything great with your lesser abilities anyway so why even make the effort.* Then fear of failure kept him from trying. When Jesus decided to travel, Isaac was in limbo again, wondering what to do. After weeks of ponderous soul-searching, he made his first major decision on his own, and decided to stay home. While organizing a future without Jesus, rebellion lost its appeal—so there he was wondering where else he would find enthusiasm. After several futile attempts to reinvolve himself, he thought *I can't find what I need because Jesus has again changed his mind about what it's wise to invest in.*

But Jesus tended to change his mind without Isaac or anyone else knowing what he was up to. He was peripatetic while at the same time incredibly thorough in terms of insight. He never stayed in unproductive thought for the sake of others and never left a thought until he understood it.

In fact Jesus was so wrapped up in his own need for knowledge that he was often hard to befriend. Then his intensity attracted the same in others. After he accepted himself for who he was and what he had to offer, he found the same friendly heart in those around him.

Did Jesus let people take advantage of him?

He went through that stage and so did Isaac. In fact they went through it together as each of them tried to live in sovereign thought.

What does sovereign mean in this reference?

A sovereign country is one that rules itself, and the same is true for you. But sovereignty isn't found by sacrificing what's important. It's found by doing what you love, thereby taking your gift to a higher level of divinity. As you do, you inspire others to do the same.

In an effort to live that sovereignty, Isaac became an Essene; a lonely existence, but one that brought him back to his principles and what he considered important: reform. As an Essene, he was happy to be with other like-minded souls but he had some adjusting to do. Using his kinship with Jesus to promote himself within the brotherhood made him very unpopular. He rationalized this predicament, as he always did, saying that Jesus resurrected and he was his cousin. Therefore others should listen to him.

Does each soul have a specific goal while here?

Each soul has specific growth it wants to embrace and each soul chooses a path that has it.

What growth am I after, Charlie?

Whatever your soul brings to you to deal with.

Is the soul looking for light?

The soul *is* light but you can't recognize that radiance until you know it's yours to shine. When Isaac finally knew what he wanted—a path of solitary prayer—resistance came from every side. He had floundered around from pursuit to pursuit for so many years, always tagging along behind somebody, that no one took him seriously. He had to dig in and get tenacious to live his heart's desire.

People said to themselves *why should we believe that Isaac has finally found his purpose simply because he's announced a new one?* Perseverance paid off, however, and he enjoyed the fruits of his labors as soon as he held them in high esteem. The building he prayed in wasn't any big strong fortress to guarantee his privacy. He had to respect his need to have it before the community took him seriously. And he had to respect the needs of others before that could happen.

By the time Isaac found this calling, Jesus had left form. Nevertheless, he felt his presence powerfully. Those who knew Jesus had a lot of thinking to do after the resurrection. *What did it mean? What had he done? What could others do?* Isaac decided that if the world was indeed an illusion, he better get busy nurturing reality. Happily, nothing got rid of procrastination faster than knowing that life survived the body.

Did Isaac come to that conclusion because Jesus seemed to have accomplished eternal life from following his heart?

His accomplishment certainly challenged Isaac to consider his.

If I'd seen Jesus return with my own eyes, I'd probably feel the same.
If you need this lesson, you'll live it.

I'm a little late for Jesus.
Time doesn't exist in terms of oneness.

Are you saying that Jesus might do it again?
I'm saying that you'll accomplish eternal life one way or another—just as everyone else will.

That's a very bold statement, Charlie.
For a very bold God.

Could it happen through resurrection?
If you call resurrection the renewal of light in matter.

I'm not sure I understand what you're saying, but a giggle is bubbling up through my soul.
The giggle is your soul finding home. That's what resurrection is.

How did Jesus' picture relate to his resurrection?
The same way your picture relates to yours: by being all that it needed to be for the timely birth. Resurrection doesn't have to be intellectually understood to be physically experienced. It has to be emotionally embraced. That's why all have an equal chance to live one.

If the picture isn't supportive in terms of my goal, what is happening?
A lack of faith is happening. You haven't understood the support it offers. Everything you live is moving you onward and inward. Honor the moment. Then resurrection is.

Can resurrection happen overnight?
No mastery happens overnight.

Change happens overnight.
External pictures change overnight. Internal pictures reveal

themselves gradually, as you become accustomed to what they tell you.

Do new decisions always have love in them?

They always have information in them. Love isn't always obvious. Ego often comes up with new anger-provoking thoughts to replace old anger-provoking thoughts. Righteous indignation had Isaac so puffed up and inflated that the balloon burst in explosions of hilarity. This was his turning point. He saw himself in the person he judged. As soon as he saw how comical that other person looked—and knew that he looked the same—he sat down and laughed until he cried.

How many ways are there for enjoying the human journey?

As many ways as you see before you. Each way chosen then becomes a future possibility for further explorations into the unlimited nature of thought. When tomorrow comes, what was true yesterday has already changed and rearranged, as the atoms split to enjoy more diversity. Kinesthesia continues as it goes through yet another metamorphosis to further implode. There is no end to what can be experienced, just as there is no wrong or right way to do it. There is only that which has been done and that which will be done.

Isaac tried to identify the right way and the wrong way, the good way and the bad way, the happy way and the sad way, hoping to choose more wisely for himself. But labeling choices as one or the other was bound to put him at risk, for then he was always worried if he'd taken the wrong way, bad way, or sad way. Fortunately, he got to the point where he realized there was only *his* way.

Oneness
Is thought merging
In joyous celebration
Of God's unique ability
To express individually.

Worksheet for Chapter 14: Isaac

What are the most vital parts of your life?

What else feels vital?

Can you name anything else that feels vital?

If everything you named suddenly disappeared, what would you be left with?

If you haven't reached an answer that has to do with inner growth, keep trying.

Questions to Ponder

• Do I live to please others or do I live to please myself?

• Am I honoring all my potential and using it well, or am I yearning for more potential?

• Am I listening to the core within or listening to the chorus without?

> Oneness can include anything.
> It's simply a merger
> Of compatibly living auras.

Personal Insights

Like Isaac, I struggled to find more purpose in life, too. I was probably clingy along the way. If so, it was only because I thought I could find some answers from being around that person. If anyone feels put upon by my need to grow—and I use the present tense because emotions have a way of sticking around—I humbly beg your forgiveness. I didn't intend to be burdensome; I only wanted to explore my possibilities and know why I was here. I tripped and stumbled like Isaac and, yes, just as people said about him—*what in the world is he up to now*—they said about me. But these days, I'm grateful that I followed my curiosity wherever it took me because, as Charlie always tells me, *it doesn't matter how long it takes you to learn what you need to learn, it only matters that you do.*

15

Leah: The Struggling Cousin

Take your belief
In the freedom of choice
And choose to love.
Otherwise,
Life becomes a series
Of undesirable mirrors
As you choose something else.

Who was Leah, Charlie?
She was the granddaughter of Mumu's sister and second cousin to Jesus.

From your phrase above, are you saying that Leah had trouble choosing love?
Yes. She chose hate because it seemed more appropriate.

It's hard to love when you feel that way.
Leah thought so, too, but once she fathomed why love was preferable, it got easier. And she fathomed why love was preferable from living without it.

Was Leah familiar with the mirror theory?
She was familiar with the give/receive concept as most people were who knew Jesus. But Leah didn't trust it when life felt awful. She indulged in self-pity; especially since her experience seemed to justify that feeling. Then ego had her right where it wanted her—too depressed to believe that a healing was possible anyway.

Leah knew enough about give/receive that she feared what she would discover if she actually dealt with her mirrors, but amazingly, fear went away as soon as she knew herself as the only person with whom she had to cope. Before that, she never thought of herself as accountable, so she never cared what she did.

What's the difference between being in-matter and out-of-matter in terms of growth?
Out-of-matter, it's easy to own up to your mirrors because growth is seen as benevolent. Ego can't block attachments so energy uses its mind the way God intended—as a means for treasuring the whole.

In-matter, ego tells you not to love, not to respect, and not to honor. *Don'ts are safe*, it says, *because while in them, nothing can be taken from you. Sit in do's and someone might come along and take what you've done! Then where will you be?* But ego lives in the world of things where *doing* and *getting* refer to outside gains. Ego doesn't know any other way of counting assets.

Did Leah have an easy life?
As a child, she did. At ten, her life changed dramatically when she lost the two people she loved the most in the world: her

grandparents, who had raised her from infancy. Not only was she devastated by that loss, she found herself in the role of an unwanted orphan, shunted back and forth between one relative and another, depending on who was willing to feed and house her. In every home she stayed, she could sense the added burden she was to an already struggling household.

This new and unwanted impasse stressed her to the point where she took her misery out on anyone close enough to hear her. Night after night she prayed for deliverance, but she thought of deliverance as the picture of life changing, not as her changing what she delivered.

Deep down she knew that these relatives weren't intentionally cruel, only busy people with lots on their minds and not enough insight to understand her plight. In her previous home, she'd been the apple of her grandparent's eye and the center of attention, making her rather spoiled. Now she was extra baggage and being ignored. The pain was almost more than she could bear.

Later, when Leah reflected on those years with her grandparents, she realized that even in the midst of their nurturing personalities, she focused on what she didn't have instead of what she did have, complaining daily that her *real* parents weren't around. She never appreciated how kind and concerned these people were until they were gone. Then her new guardians had to be dealt with.

What happened to her biological parents?
She never knew them. Her mother had borne her out of wedlock and was stoned to death shortly after Leah was born. Her father disappeared from her mother's life before she knew she was pregnant.

Would her life have been easier had her new guardians been kinder?
No.

Why not? A kinder person deals differently.
A kinder person meets those who deal likewise. She received the same emotional support from her new guardians that she had

given to her old guardians. Her grandparents were good to her in every way they knew how to be. They were elderly, however, and Leah wanted young and vital. She handled her disappointment badly. Even at a young age, she had a choice. She could either appreciate what she had, or she could complain about what she didn't.

Everything is so reversed in your thinking.

You mean inward instead of outward? That's the difference between illusion and reality. In reality you create from within. Leah suffered the same inverted thinking and blamed anyone she could find for her unwelcome status. When she kept that blame a personal release, she only suffered her own black moods. When she made that blame a public one, she suffered the black moods of others as well. These relatives did their best on her behalf. But as she belittled their efforts, their efforts were never enough.

Did she stay with Mary and Joseph?

Yes, and she enjoyed being there more than she did the other places she stayed. It was a busy household with lots of children and things to do.

Did she want to live there permanently?

She spoke of it, but Mary and Joseph had limited resources and felt that caring for Leah should be a shared experience with several families.

Was that better for Leah?

It was better for Leah to live with several families where the people were comfortable taking their turn than it was to live with one family where resentment was constantly present.

Why do we come into illusion to live these struggles in the first place?

You mean why do we come to the Earth experience where illusion exists? Because it's so much fun to be here while still enjoying reality. Since reality is love, this is where the focus needs to be. No one comes here in forgetfulness, however. The infant knows reality. To know it again is to live as the infant does with a heart full of love and a ready welcome to all. What prevents you from being this person?

I have reasons for being careful, reasons for doubting, and reasons for fear and rejection.
None of which the infant considers.

But the infant doesn't know enough to consider them.
How did you learn to consider them?

From experience.
What if that infant learns from experience, too, and knows that doubt, fear, and rejection only live in illusion?

Has any soul ever lived in reality the whole time it was here in the last hundred years?
Plenty of humans have remembered reality in the last hundred years. To find an adult who never struggled through illusion first you'd have to go further back. However, there was a time when energy lived in perpetual love. It happened for the same reason it happens today: life is appreciated for what it is.

Leah's struggles all began with the following: *Why aren't they doing this instead of that? Why aren't they saying this instead of that? Why aren't they giving this instead of that?* As she put these questions to others, they became her own. Yes, loving ideas are easier to remember when they're being talked about, but they're being talked about when they're being lived. The more they're being lived the more they're being enjoyed.

Leah's attitude was *why should I care? I'm poor, discarded, and unappreciated, and no one deserves my love.* It was her way of protecting her feelings, but it kept her focused on all that was wrong. With a focus on the negative, she never acknowledged her gift here on Earth. Had she welcomed and embraced that gift, she would have used it. Using it would have expanded it. Expanding it would have made her welcome into these households instead of

merely tolerated. Had she been more productive in these shel-
tered environments early in life, she would have had the skills she
needed later to enter the world at large and become a useful member of society. Instead she shunned and devalued the gift.

Leah had a gift that would have supported her?

Sure. Doesn't everyone have a wonderful way of loving others
and supporting his or her journey?

Like a job or a career?

Sometimes. Doesn't your job or career support you? And
doesn't it bring an offering to others?

Didn't she eventually marry and have a husband to support her?

No, Leah never married, but even had she, her husband's gift
wouldn't have brought her the same satisfaction that honoring her
own would have. She had to value her gift and expand it. With all
the pooh-poohing she did regarding its value, she didn't want to
own what she belittled.

*Why didn't she just behave like "out-of-matter" energy and have that be her
mirror.*

How do you perceive out-of-matter energy as behaving?

It doesn't expect reward, does it?

Only because it understands the nature of reward—the mirror
of its own beloved heart. The only difference between giving in-
matter and giving out-of-matter is matter. You're in a game where
matter is relevant regarding your gift. Leah is now in a game where
it isn't. Therefore each of you is living the game of choice for the
moment. After feeling the fun of knowing yourself out-of-matter,
you want to know yourself in-matter, too. As you learn the true
nature of your energy, you add *matter skills* to your already masterful aura.

Was Leah close to Jesus while growing up?

They enjoyed growth together, both after they came and before they arrived. Mirrors have a way of tagging along after each other out-of-matter, too. So while Jesus was busy planning his Earthly journey, Leah was busy planning hers. For the duration, both of them tried to honor the gifts seeded beforehand. At any given moment, Jesus had the same respect for Leah's gift that he had for his. He was challenged to honor his essence just as much as Leah was challenged to honor hers. Sometimes he did, sometimes he didn't. But to know God's help, he had to trust his mirror. If no one in humanness had his mirror, out-of-matter energy reflected it. God provided regardless.

Can a mirror be someone more evolved?

The level of evolvement is irrelevant. As you love, you are loved.

What kind of healing did Leah experience this lifetime?

It happened through the disease of leprosy. Devastated when she got it, she thought to herself, *too young to die, too young to move to the leper's colony, too young to lose any hope of a happy tomorrow.* She tried to contact Jesus but he was away on one of his frequent journeys around the provinces. So she moved to the colony and did the best she could to cope.

When Jesus returned and came to see her, he wasn't upset at all. He was calm, gracious, and confident that all was going to be fine. Grateful for his reassurance, Leah made an effort to look at her predicament in the best possible light. The first thing that struck her was the lack of adequate shelter. People were wandering around in a daze; the very sick and the not so sick together, looking for someone to help them. Then and there she decided to organize some kind of permanent refuge where the needs of the lepers could be met with more consistency. Soon she had a very active post and two assistants.

Slowly but surely the essence in her reawakened. With her vivid lesson of what it meant to face adversity unprepared, she was able to help the ill-prepared in the colony to face this new and unwanted challenge. Gradually the outside picture of illness began to lose importance as the inside feeling of love transformed her life. The more she tended the sick and bewildered, the less bewildered she felt.

Others saw Leah as this healer at a very young age, but she alone had to own this quality, take responsibility for having it, and use it in a way that she enjoyed. Her soul had gotten her into a situation where she either had to use her gift, or sit down and die. She chose to use it. As a result, love filled her heart to such an extent that the body began to reflect her new and enlightened focus. With all the ease she was finding from spreading more love around, dis-ease had no room in which to be. Much to her surprise and delight, she stayed in this beautiful pause of remission long enough to have a child, and long enough to love Naomi through her infancy.

Wasn't it foolish to have a child who would probably get sick?

It may have seemed foolish to others. To her it felt like the heart of God in remembrance of self—her mirror.

What inspired Leah to have Naomi?

Love for herself and Naomi's father.

Is that enough?

I believe so. Naomi's decision to come here and live her beautiful journey proved to be so loving a choice that she lived her own resurrection, too. And she lived it as well and as fully as Jesus lived his. Once you feel what it means to be this God in the wonderful game of humanness, you can fall back on that memory any time you wish to.

What's a good reason for falling back on it?

Helping others to fall back on theirs. Have faith in the person you are and appreciate the gift of your presence here. Then you'll live as Naomi did. Yes, she contacted leprosy from exposure to the disease but her heart was too big to keep it. When she saw the love in Jesus' soul, she opted for his belief instead of Leah's.

Jesus didn't believe in death anymore. Leah still did. On one of his many visits to the colony, he and Leah were sitting quietly one afternoon when Naomi slipped off her lap and onto his. They looked into each other's eyes while chatting playfully and, as Naomi came back to Leah, her body went from sickness to health right before her eyes. Leah couldn't believe what she was seeing. Darkness fell away as light encircled Naomi. The radiance of her aura almost blinded Leah. Of course she was ecstatic, and in her new moment of exhilarating health, Naomi was, too.

Then it occurred to Leah. Naomi had healed. And because she had, she couldn't stay in the colony. What a catastrophe! At first she was beside herself. History was repeating itself. Once again, she was losing the most important person in her life. This time, however, she knew the magnitude of her loss.

In the weeks that followed, Leah wavered back and forth between absolute devastation and total bliss. Since she couldn't find the same reality Naomi had, she couldn't live where Naomi was. That was wrenching. But she knew that Naomi had lived a miracle and if Naomi had, she could, too. That was exhilarating. Therefore, Leah lived a constant vigil of trying to focus on the benefits of what had happened instead of the losses.

Jesus was a great help, too, praising her gift and reminding her that this was the source of love. He saw leprosy as the miracle revealing her gift. She had lived whatever she needed in order to find it. He never pitied her because he didn't think pity was appropriate. Leah was more vibrant after coming to the colony than she'd ever been before. He saw her as a light getting brighter and he saw that radiance as the only prognosis of consequence.

Had Leah honored her gift earlier, would she have gotten sick?

The soul is always living the momentary wisdom. What *is* is the pertinent love.

Wouldn't she have had a longer life had she not gotten leprosy?

Perhaps, but a long life was not the goal. The goal was to find her God-giving soul in the time she had. Whatever reawakened that beauty was the path of longevity.

After Naomi left, Leah survived long enough to hear that Naomi was turning into a lovely young girl, and long enough to feel joyful that it was so. Naomi wasn't encouraged to visit but Leah understood and blessed her journey. Not that she didn't wallow in self-pity on occasion, she did. But using her gift brought enormous satisfaction and bemoaning her losses didn't, so she used her determination to stay as focused as possible. As appreciation for the gift grew, Leah was able to support herself for the first time in her life. Nursing was a talent in great demand in a leper colony.

Was leprosy greatly shunned by society?
Only in that those who had it were isolated from those who didn't.

Did Leah feel unloved because of her quarantine?
She felt unloved when she didn't love. After moving to the colony she spent her days making sure that others were comfortable. Therefore, comfort was hers. The lepers had visitors, though. They weren't completely isolated. Jesus and several of his friends, who understood the source of fear and never did anything to bring it upon themselves, welcomed the chance to be useful. They knew that to go beyond fear was to go beyond finite thought and to live in the love they hoped to encounter in others.

How was Leah different before her illness as opposed to afterward?
Before, she refused to take responsibility for her life and the many woes that resulted. Afterward, she praised the circumstances that had helped her to find her gift. Before, she lived off the goodness of others. Afterward, she lived whatever would reveal her own true goodness. I'm not saying that the people who took care of Leah early in her life were not a blessing, they were. They kept her alive long enough so that Leah could search for benevolence. But the soul can't rest easy while thinking that survival is up to the whims of others.

Leah lived most of her life without a place where she belonged or one that truly belonged to her. After going to the colony, she had her first permanent address. Amazingly, that trauma was the very incentive she needed. It pushed her to set up a space of her own within the community, a place where her personality and hopes and dreams could be showcased, and a place where she could be the hostess and caregiver. This was an opportunity she'd never had before. Leah used to say that she wasn't savvy enough to take care of herself. But the truth is that she only had to respect her gift and nurture it. Then as she brought it lovingly to others, the universe could support her in whatever way she needed.

Had Leah ever been in love before she came to the colony?
No. It was only after she found her giving heart that she learned what love truly meant.

How could it matter at that late date?
The very illness that Leah thought would kill her prematurely was the very miracle that enabled her to live forever, in- and out-of-form, whenever she wished to. She went from a life of extreme poverty to a life of total awareness as she went from begging God for a meal to begging God for eternity. Because she kept her focus on the absolute and where it resided, everything it held was hers to enjoy. Nothing changed on the outside; the miracle was within. Later, as the body sensed the end of its journey, it merely needed a quick reminder to jump back into the awareness the rest of her understood.

Why couldn't she heal on the outside, too, and come back as Jesus did?
It didn't feel like a loving choice, and nothing is a gift if the giver isn't loved in the process.

Others might have seen the power of love.
Others would have seen her giving it up. Use your own life as an example. Are you so happy to make decisions based on the possible growth spurts of others? Carry this thought with you as you nourish your stay.
The human journey is a search for deeper love. Giving up your pleasures won't help you to find it no matter how many good reasons you give yourself for living in denial. Others need to see you living autonomous beauty because this is the inspiration they need for liv-

ing in theirs. Leah learned this wisdom from deciding that she deserved the heaven of her own reward as much as Jesus deserved his.

Did she always love Jesus?

No more than she was able to love herself, and the same was true for him.

If you had to sum up the one thing Jesus said that meant the most to Leah, what would it be?

That he and she were one.

From this story, it seems that Leah's choices paid off for her.

Indeed they did. In her youth, she had all the trappings of material comfort and every reason to appreciate life, but didn't. In her final years she had all the trappings of poverty, and every reason to be miserable, but wasn't. In between she longed to feel connected to the people around her, but couldn't. Not until the ravages of disease irreversibly changed her life did the balm of healing begin. Then she realized how health and wholeness hadn't come from the picture rearranging; it had come from the rearranging of inner thought. Sickness hadn't made Leah miserable any more than fitness had made her happy. How she felt in each determined her mood.

When all was said and done, she wouldn't have changed a moment of that history; for the living of these extremes spoke to her as nothing else could have. Had she not experienced the ease and comfort that should have made her blissful—and didn't, or the sickness and loss that should have made her miserable—and hadn't, she wouldn't have recognized the love and compassion that helped her to know herself.

> If you want the picture of life to please you,
> Notice the feeling it offers.
> This is the reality that stays around
> Long after the picture has joined oblivion.

Worksheet for Chapter 15: Leah

Write down all the people who have disappointed you in your life.

In one or two words, write down how they disappointed you.

In each situation, what did that disappointment help you to understand?

Which of those instances were major growth spurts?

List all the ways you can thank these people for pushing you to become a deeper, more compassionate person.

Questions to Ponder

• Am I giving the love I long for or am I always waiting for others to love me first?

• Do I pray for more happiness or do I pray for ways of making others happy?

• Am I holding up my martyr's foil for all to see or am I taking responsibility as the maker of my destiny?

> If you try to fulfill your longings
> With illusionary reward,
> The heart goes bankrupt.

Personal Insights

For a long time, I shared Leah's belief that some of my early influences had been detrimental to my growth. I, too, blamed that uneasiness on the circumstances beyond my control. I also felt that my life would have gone more smoothly had the nurturing I needed been there as a child. I ignored my gift when it revealed itself early in life, as Leah did, but just as she blossomed spiritually, emotionally, and even physically after she honored her gift, so did my life blossom when reverence was brought to mine. Just as the universe handled Leah's needs after she brought her gift to others, so has the universe blessed me with what I need.

I leave you temporarily with a reminder that I hear so often from Charlie: Trust in the moment and find what is good about it, for the moment is all you have.

Light has no particular look.
But the more you love your
Particulars,
The lighter you become.
The lighter you become,
The more you live in love.
The more you live in love,
The more you face that love in others.
As the process accelerates,
The soul becomes too big to live in one place
And therefore lives in every place.

Endnotes

1. The Holy Bible, Kings James Version (Nashville: Broadman & Holman Publishers, 1979).

2. While he yet talked to the people, behold, his mother and his brothers stood without, desiring to speak to him. (Matt. 12:46)

Then they said unto him, Behold, thy mother and thy brethren stand without, desiring to speak with thee. (Matt. 12:47)

There came then his brethren and his mother, and, standing without, sent unto him, calling him. And the multitude sat about him, and they said unto him, Behold, thy mother and thy brethren without seek for thee. (Mark 3:31–32)

But he, [Peter] beckoning unto them with the hand to hold the peace, declared unto them how the Lord had brought him out of the prison. And he said, Go shew these things unto James, and to the brethren. And he departed, and went unto another place. (Acts 12:17)

And after they had held their peace, James answered, saying Men *and* brethren, hearken unto me. (Acts 15:13)

Then came to him [Jesus] his mother and his brethren, and could not come at him for the press. (Luke 8:19)

And it was told him by certain which said, Thy mother and thy brethren stand without, desiring to see thee. (Luke 8:20)

After this he [Jesus] went down to Capernaum, he, and his mother, and his brethren, and his disciples: and they continued there not many days. (John 2:12)

And they said, Is not this Jesus, the son of Joseph, whose father and mother we know? how is it then that he saith, I came down from heaven? (John 6:42)

His brethren therefore said unto him, Depart hence, and go unto Judaea, that thy disciples also may see the works that thou doest. (John 7:3)

For neither did his brethren believe in him. (John 7:5)

But when his brethren were gone up, then went he also up into the feast, not openly, but as it were in secret. (John 7:10)

Have we not power to lead about a sister, a wife, as well as other apostles, and as the brethren of the Lord, and Cephas? (Corinthians 9:5)

3. Tertullian (c160–c255), *Against Marcion* (Milano, Italy: Vanese, Istituto editoriale cisalpino, 1971) and http://www.geocities.com/paulntobin/james-brother.html.

4. Hershel Shanks, *Understanding the Dead Sea Scrolls* (New York: Random House, 1992): p. 285.

5. Millar Burrows, *Burrows on the Dead Sea Scrolls* (Baker Book House with permission of Viking Penguin, 1978): p. 17.

6. Flavius Josephus, "Antiquities of the Jews." *The Complete Works of Flavius Josephus* (Grand Rapids: Kregel Publications, 1960): p. 423.

7. Laurence Gardner, *Bloodline of the Holy Grail: The Hidden Lineage of Jesus Revealed* (Gloucester, Mass.: Fair Winds Press, 2002): p. 11.

8. Ibid., p. 28.

9. John Rousseau and Rami Arav, *Jesus and His World* (Minneapolis: Augsburg Fortress, 1995): p. 352.

10. *The Panarion and Ancoratus of Epiphanius* (http://graal.co.uk/ossuary.html).

11. Andre Lemaire, "Burial Box of James the Brother of Jesus." *Biblical Archaeology Review*, vol. 28 (November/December, 2002): pp. 24–33.

12. Hershel Shanks and Ben Witherington III, *The Brother of Jesus: The Dramatic Story & Meaning of the First Archaeological Link to Jesus and His Family* (San Francisco: HarperCollins Publishers, 2003): Introduction part 1, p. xii; and "The Story of James, Son of Joseph, Brother of Jesus": part 2, p. 245.

13. Ibid., p. 25.

14. Ibid., pp. 168–169.

15. Ibid., pp. 207–208.

16. Eusebius (c260–c340), *The History of the Church* (Baltimore: Penguin Books, 1965): p. 58.

17. Ibid., p. 81.

18. Robert Eisenman, *James, The Brother of Jesus: The Key to Unlocking the Secrets of Early Christianity and the Dead Sea Scrolls* (New York: Penguin Books, 1998): Introduction p. xvii.

19. Ibid., p. 8.

20. Ibid., p. 33.

21. Ibid., p. 74.

22. Ibid., p. 771.

23. Ibid., p. 753.

24. Gardner, *Bloodline of the Holy Grail*, p. 118.

25. Eisenman, *James, The Brother of Jesus*, p. xviii.

About the Author

Bader Howar Photography

Betsy Thompson is a Philadelphia native with a B.F.A. from the University of Pennsylvania. She has worked in radio and acted in television commercials in Philadelphia and New York, and has been working in the motion picture business for the past seventeen years in Los Angeles.

She published and distributed the following four books through her own company, Ascension Publishing: *Loveparent: How to Be the Parent You Hope to Be; Lovehuman: How to Be Who You Love; You Are What You Think: Make Your Thoughts Delicious,* and *The What Happens If I . . . Book: How to Make Action/Reaction Work for You Instead of Against You.*

Betsy has four children: Trace DeHaven, a civil servant in Olympia, Washington; Elizabeth Glass, a jeweler in Walton, New York; Catherine Peace Victorson, a homemaker in Baltimore, Maryland; and Bill DeHaven, a furniture maker in Perkasie, Pennsylvania. She lives in Burbank, California.